DK Pock...

W9-AYS-150

ANCIENT ROME

FACTS AT YOUR FINGERTIPS

LONDON, NEW YORK, MUNICH,
MELBOURNE, and DELHI

DK DELHI
Senior editor Shatarupa Chaudhuri
Assistant editor Priyanka Kharbanda
Art editors Nishesh Batnagar, Isha Nagar, Amit Varma
DTP designers Syed Md Farhan, Jaypal Singh Chauhan
Picture researcher Aditya Katyal
Managing editor Alka Thakur
Managing art editor Romi Chakraborty
CTS manager Balwant Singh
Production manager Pankaj Sharma

DK LONDON
Senior editor Rob Houston
US editor Margaret Parrish
Senior art editor Spencer Holbrook
Managing editor Gareth Jones
Managing art editor Philip Letsu
Jacket editor Manisha Majithia
Jacket designers Laura Brim, Nishesh Batnagar
Jacket design development manager
Sophia M. Tampakopoulos Turner
Producer (pre-production) Rebecca Fallowfield
Producer (print production) Mary Slater
Publisher Andrew Macintyre
Associate publishing director Liz Wheeler
Art director Phil Ormerod
Publishing director Jonathan Metcalf
Consultant Philip Parker

First American Edition, 2014
Published in the United States by DK Publishing
4th floor, 345 Hudson Street, New York, New York 10014

14 15 16 17 10 9 8 7 6 5 4 3 2 1
001–187500–June/14

Copyright © 2014 Dorling Kindersley Limited
A Penguin Company
All rights reserved. Without limiting the rights under copyright
reserved above, no part of this publication may be reproduced,
stored in or introduced into a retrieval system, or transmitted, in
any form, or by any means (electronic, mechanical, photocopying,
recording, or otherwise), without the prior written permission of
both the copyright owner and the above publisher of this book.
Published in Great Britain by Dorling Kindersley Limited.

A catalog record for this book is available from
the Library of Congress.
ISBN: 978-1-4654-2013-8

Printed and bound by South China
Printing Company, China

**Discover more at
www.dk.com**

CONTENTS

4 Roman Republic
6 Roman Empire
8 Later Roman Empire
10 Trade and transportation

 14 ANCIENT ROMANS

16 Roman society
18 Emperors and leaders
28 Soldiers and generals
30 Nobles
34 Thinkers
36 Slaves
38 Gladiators

40 THE MILITARY

42 Roman army
44 Weapons
48 Uniform and armor
54 Roman wars
56 Wars and battles
62 Enemies

 66 RELIGION

68 Religious beliefs
70 Gods

80 BUILDINGS AND MONUMENTS

82 Cities
86 Architecture
88 Homes
90 Temples
98 Villas and palaces
100 Baths
102 Open-air arenas
108 Aqueducts

112 ROMAN LIFE

114 Daily life
116 At work
118 Writing
120 In the house
124 Dressing up
128 Medicine
130 Entertainment
132 Toys and games
136 Music
138 Arts and crafts
140 Works of art

146 At a glance
148 Numbers and letters
150 Glossary
152 Index
156 Acknowledgments

Scales and sizes

This book contains profiles of ancient Roman artifacts with scale drawings to indicate their size.

 6 ft (1.8 m)

 6 in (15 cm)

Locator

A red shaded area shows the region of a war. A red dot marks the location of a Roman site.

Roman Republic

For centuries after Rome was founded in 753 BCE, it was just a small town in central Italy. At first ruled by kings, but later becoming a Republic, it conquered its neighbors and then faraway lands over time to become the greatest power in the Mediterranean.

Romulus and Remus with she-wolf

Legendary founders

According to legend, Rome was founded by Romulus, son of the war god Mars. He, along with his brother Remus, was brought up by a she-wolf.

Tarquinius Superbus

Roman kings

Romulus was first of the seven kings of Rome. The last king, Tarquinius Superbus, was a tyrant. He was eventually overthrown after an uprising in 510 BCE, following which the Roman people set up a republic.

Senators

The Republic

From 510 BCE, Rome became a Republic, governed by the Senate—a group of elected noblemen. During its lifetime—nearly 500 years until civil wars led to its collapse—official documents carried the initials SPQR ("the Senate and the People of Rome").

SPQR inscribed on an ancient Roman coin

Senate and society

Originally, the men in the Senate (senators) were mostly rich Romans called "patricians." Gradually the poorer people, called plebeians, managed to get some of this power for themselves.

Neighbors

Rome united the region of Italy under its rule by conquering its neighbors, such as the Latins, Samnites, and Etruscans (seen in this painting). Later it defeated the Carthaginians of North Africa in three wars (264–146 BCE) to become rulers of the Mediterranean region.

Roman Empire

Empires are controlled by absolute rulers called emperors, and in 27 BCE, the Roman Republic became an empire. At that time, it had armies that were more powerful than its neighbors, prosperous cities, and a language, Latin, spoken by millions.

End of the Republic

A series of civil wars after 100 BCE tore the Republic apart. An army general, Julius Caesar won one of these, but was assassinated in 44 BCE. After the sea battle of Actium in 31 BCE, his adoptive son Octavian finally emerged as the victor.

Roman legionaries (soldiers) aboard ship

Roman warship

Roman Empire around 250 CE

The first emperor

In 27 BCE, Octavian was awarded the title Augustus by the Senate and became emperor. Although there were still consuls, they no longer exercised any real power.

Expansion

The early Roman emperors pushed the frontier toward the Rhine and Danube rivers to expand the empire's borders. In 43 CE, Emperor Claudius began the conquest of Britain. By the time of the death of Emperor Trajan in 117 CE, the empire had reached its greatest extent.

Godlike status

The emperors had supreme power. After their deaths, some of them, especially Augustus, were regarded as gods, and temples were set up in their honor. This picture of an altar shows Emperor Antoninus Pius becoming a god.

Later Roman Empire

By the 3rd century CE, the Roman Empire had stopped expanding, weakened by a series of civil wars and rebellions. It took strong emperors to restore order and reform the empire, but invasions in the 5th century made it weak again.

Tetrarchy

Over time it became difficult for one man to govern the large Roman Empire. In 293 CE, Emperor Diocletian solved this problem by establishing a system called the tetrarchy in which four emperors, or "tetrarchs," shared power.

Statue of tetrarchs

Arrival of Christianity

At first, Christianity was practiced as a secret cult. Christians, if discovered, were persecuted. In 313 CE, however, Emperor Constantine made the religion legal throughout the empire. After him, almost all Roman emperors were Christian.

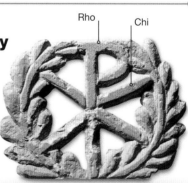

Rho

Chi

Christian chi-rho symbol

Invasions

From the mid-3rd century, raids by tribes living outside the Roman frontier increased. Despite the efforts of Roman generals, such as Stilicho, the borders collapsed around 400 CE. Tribes such as the Goths, Vandals, and Franks took over most of Rome's western provinces.

Diptych of Stilicho

Division of the Empire

From 395 CE, the western and eastern provinces of the Roman Empire had separate rulers. In 476 CE the last western emperor was overthrown, but under strong rulers, such as Justinian, the eastern empire survived another 1,000 years.

Emperor Justinian

Trade and transportation

Rome's vast empire created a huge trading industry that flourished over land and sea. Essentials, such as olive oil, wine, and grain, and luxuries, such as glass, were traded within the empire. Slaves, spices, and exotic animals were imported from outside the empire's borders.

Building roads

Roman engineers built a network of roads across the empire. These high-quality roads were made of layers of crushed stone and gravel topped with flat slabs, and they helped transport goods over land with ease.

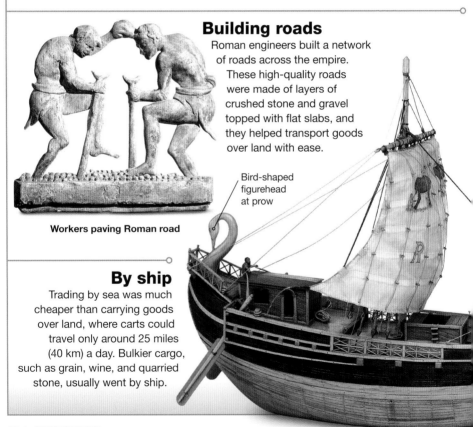

Workers paving Roman road

Bird-shaped figurehead at prow

By ship

Trading by sea was much cheaper than carrying goods over land, where carts could travel only around 25 miles (40 km) a day. Bulkier cargo, such as grain, wine, and quarried stone, usually went by ship.

Trade items

Merchants carried various items, such as lumber from Lebanon, granite from Egypt, pottery from Gaul (France), and grain, olive oil, and wine from North Africa. Liquids were carried in *amphorae* (jars).

The shape of *amphorae* made it easy to pack them tightly

Coinage

Coins bearing the head of the emperor were circulated throughout the empire as the common currency. Under the early empire, one gold *aureus* was equivalent to 25 silver *denarii*.

Aureus

Denarius

Sesterius (bronze coin)

Industry

Over time, products such as high-grade pottery from Gaul, Rhineland glass, and North African fish sauce were developed on a large scale. The Romans also built grand structures using complex cranes and pulleys.

Crane used in building construction

The Romans built more than
250,000 miles
(400,000 km) of roads, with the longest road stretching over 930 miles (1,500 km)

SYSTEM OF ROADS

Roman roads were famous for being absolutely straight. They were usually lined on top with paving stones. There were different types of road, such as highways and city streets. This Roman road in Jerash, Jordan, is a *cardo maximus*, which was the main road in a Roman city. It is lined with columns with an arched gateway at the end, but these were not usual features.

Ancient Romans

Roman society had a strict ranking system, depending on whether the people in the empire were citizens or noncitizens, how rich or poor they were, and what official jobs they held. People of different classes could even be identified by their clothing. During the Roman Empire, the emperor held the highest position. This carving shows a procession in honor of Emperor Augustus.

TREASURY
This carving of a money bag is inscribed with "traveler to the *aerarium*." The empire's wealth was stored in an *aerarium* (or treasury).

Roman society

From the beginning, the Roman Republic had strict social divisions between privileged patricians and poorer plebeians. Most people did not have full Roman citizenship and so had fewer legal rights than those who did.

Military diploma granting citizenship

Citizens

The most common ways to gain Roman citizenship were by joining a city council or by serving 25 years as a Roman auxiliary (noncitizen) soldier.

Mother watching her children play

Families

The eldest man in a family, or *paterfamilias*, was the head of the household and had authority over all. Women could not hold office, but could run businesses. Children had to obey their elders, or face the risk of being thrown out of the home.

Thinking minds

Learning flourished under the empire, with fine poets such as Virgil, historians such as Plutarch (seen in this 17th-century fresco), and philosophers such as Seneca.

Class structure

In the days of the empire, senators had the most political power after the emperor. Equestrians held lesser government positions or were businessmen. With some rights and often their own businesses, freed slaves were slightly better off than slaves, who were at the bottom of the social order and had almost no rights.

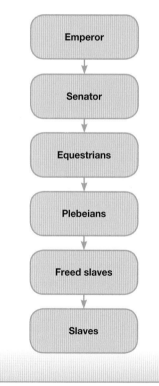

Emperor
↓
Senator
↓
Equestrians
↓
Plebeians
↓
Freed slaves
↓
Slaves

FOCUS ON...
ROYAL SYMBOLS
Some elements in an emperor's wardrobe set him apart.

▲ Emperors wore wreaths of laurel leaves, called *corona triumphalis*, instead of crowns.

▲ Only an emperor could wear clothes that were entirely purple. The purple dye was made by boiling *Murex* sea snails.

Emperors and leaders

Power struggles weakened the Senate and Rome passed under the rule of emperors. The emperors did not share power with the Senate and ruled independently.

Julius Caesar

One of Rome's most able generals, Julius Caesar conquered many lands, such as Gaul. After winning the Great Roman Civil War (49 45 BCE), he declared himself a dictator—an absolute or sole ruler. He played a large part in turning the Republic into what was to become the Roman Empire.

FULL NAME
Gaius Julius Caesar

LIVED c. 100–44 BCE

IN OFFICE
45–44 BCE

TITLE
Dictator

Mark Antony

After a period of struggle that followed Caesar's death, Antony and Octavian, Caesar's adopted son, gained power. But conflict between the two led to war and Antony joined forces with the Egyptian queen Cleopatra. He was eventually defeated and committed suicide.

FULL NAME
Marcus Antonius

LIVED 83–30 BCE

IN OFFICE 44–33 BCE

TITLE Consul

Livia

Married to Emperor Augustus for 51 years, Livia had great political power. After her death, she was named Diva Augusta (the Divine Augusta) and declared a goddess.

FULL NAME Livia Drusilla

LIVED 58 BCE–29 CE

IN OFFICE 27 BCE–14 CE

TITLE Empress

Augustus

After a period of civil war, Octavian became the absolute ruler of Rome, and the Senate gave him the title of Augustus, meaning "venerable." He became the first emperor, bringing an end to the Republic era.

1st-century CE cameo, or carving, of Augustus

FULL NAME Gaius Julius Caesar Octavianus

LIVED 63 BCE–14 CE

IN OFFICE 27 BCE–14 CE

TITLE Emperor

Frame added in 18th century CE

Caligula

Gaius earned the nickname Caligula (Little Boots) when he went on campaigns as a child. Historians believe he was an insane ruler who thought he was god.

FULL NAME
Gaius Julius Caesar Augustus Germanicus

LIVED 12–41 CE

IN OFFICE 37–41 CE

TITLE Emperor

Agrippina

Exiled after plotting to murder her brother, Caligula, Agrippina married Claudius, her uncle. She persuaded him to make her son, Nero, his heir. Nero, considered to have been mentally unstable by historians, later sent assassins to kill her.

FULL NAME Julia Augusta Agrippina

LIVED 15–59 CE

IN OFFICE
49–54 CE

TITLE
Empress

Claudius

Claudius was kept out of politics by his family because of his physical disabilities. When he came to power, however, he proved to be a good administrator and conquered new territories for Rome.

FULL NAME
Tiberius Claudius Caesar Augustus Germanicus

LIVED c. 10 BCE–54 CE

IN OFFICE 41–54 CE

TITLE Emperor

Nero

Nero created Coenatio Rotunda, a rotating dining room, in his villa Golden House.

Nero ruled well for the first five years of his reign, helped by advisers, including his tutor, Seneca. His lasting reputation, however, has been that of a brutal ruler who persecuted Christians. Following an uprising, he committed suicide to avoid being assassinated.

FULL NAME Nero Claudius Caesar Augustus Germanicus

LIVED 37–68 CE

IN OFFICE 54–68 CE

TITLE Emperor

Vespasian

After becoming emperor, Vespasian was able to establish some stability and end the civil wars that followed Nero's death. He was the first Roman emperor to have his son as a direct successor. This 17th-century CE painting shows Vespasian ordering the construction of the famous arena, the Colosseum.

FULL NAME Titus Flavius Caesar Vespasianus Augustus

LIVED 9–79 CE

IN OFFICE 69–79 CE

TITLE Emperor

Trajan

A general before he became emperor, Trajan took many territories, such as Dacia. Toward the end of his rule, he conquered much of Parthia, including Mesopotamia, helping the Roman Empire reach its greatest size. He also commissioned many public buildings in Rome.

FULL NAME	Caesar Nerva Traianus Augustus
LIVED	c. 53–117 CE
IN OFFICE	98–117 CE
TITLE	Emperor

Trajan's Market in Rome was a two-story market complex with more than 150 stores.

Hadrian

Most Roman emperors did not venture much outside modern-day Italy, but Hadrian traveled extensively around the empire. He was a good leader and started many building and defense works—such as the construction of Hadrian's Wall—to establish the empire's borders.

FULL NAME	Caesar Traianus Hadrianus Augustus
LIVED	76–138 CE
IN OFFICE	117–138 CE
TITLE	Emperor

Antoninus Pius

After taking the throne, Antoninus saved the senators sentenced to death by his adoptive father, Hadrian. He collected taxes to fund schools, repair public buildings, and improve trade and transportation.

FULL NAME	Titus Aelius Hadrianus Antoninus Augustus Pius
LIVED	86–161 CE
IN OFFICE	138–161 CE
TITLE	Emperor

Marcus Aurelius

The reign of Marcus Aurelius was marked by wars in Asia against the Parthian Empire and in the northern provinces against Germanic tribes. He was also a philosopher and wrote a series called *Meditations* while on his military campaigns.

FULL NAME Caesar Marcus Aurelius Antoninus Augustus

LIVED 121–180 CE

IN OFFICE 161–180 CE

TITLE Emperor

20th-century replica of an ancient Roman statue

Septimius Severus

Severus rose to fame as a general and provincial governor. He was declared emperor in 193 CE but then had to defeat political rivals to secure his position. He increased the army's pay and set up three new legions (army units), adding to both the power as well as the expense of the Roman army.

FULL NAME Caesar Lucius Septimius Severus Pertinax Augustus

LIVED 145–211 CE

IN OFFICE 193–211 CE

TITLE Emperor

Diocletian

After a successful military career, Diocletian ran the government with the discipline of an army general. He was also famous for persecuting Christians. After introducing tetrarchy (see p. 8), he felt the empire was so stable that he went into retirement in his palace in Split, Croatia.

FULL NAME
Gaius Aurelius Valerius Diocletianus Augustus

LIVED 245–313 CE

IN OFFICE 284–305 CE

TITLE Emperor

Constantine I

When Constantine I came to the throne, the empire was divided into two halves—East and West. He reunited the empire, although it later split again, and he was the first Christian emperor. This 20th-century statue of Constantine was erected in York, England—the city where he had been hailed as emperor.

FULL NAME Flavius Valerius Constantinus Augustus

LIVED 272–337 CE

IN OFFICE 306–337 CE

TITLE Emperor

Valentinian I

A soldier in his early life, Valentinian set about fortifying Rome's borders after becoming the emperor. This 16th-century illustration of Valentinian is based on Roman coins.

FULL NAME Flavius Valentinianus Augustus

LIVED 321–375 CE

IN OFFICE 360–375 CE

TITLE Emperor

Theodosius I

Also called Theodosius the Great, he was the last emperor to rule over both Western and Eastern Empires of Rome. He passed decrees to make Christianity the state religion. This bust is displayed in Spain, his birthplace.

FULL NAME Flavius Theodosius Augustus

LIVED 347–395 CE

IN OFFICE 379–395 CE

TITLE Emperor

At 73 miles (117 km), Hadrian's Wall took
15,000 workers
six to seven years to build

HADRIAN'S WALL
Emperor Hadrian built a wall from the east to the west coast of Roman Britain to guard the region against enemies. Sixteen forts and 80 milecastles (small forts) were constructed along it so that 15,000 soldiers could stay there and patrol the wall's length. These are the remains of Milecastle 39, also known as Castle Nick.

Soldiers and generals

Social class determined the ranks within the army, with the higher positions mostly reserved for men from the upper class. Often, the officers had political goals and later served society as statesmen. In the late Republic, generals came to have more power than politicians.

Scipio Africanus

This 16th-century Italian plate bears the profile of Scipio, a Roman general. He is famous for defeating Hannibal at the Second Punic War. He was given the title "Africanus" in honor of his victories in Africa, but was later accused by political rivals of taking bribes and retired to his country estate.

FULL NAME
Publius Cornelius Scipio Africanus

LIVED 236–183 BCE

IN OFFICE 210–201 BCE

ROLE General

Gaius Marius

Marius was the first consul to be elected to the office seven times. He introduced many reforms for the army. After his significant victory over the Germanic tribe the Cimbri, Marius was called "the third founder of Rome." This 19th-century painting shows him after the triumph.

Marius

FULL NAME	Gaius Marius
LIVED	157–86 BCE
IN OFFICE	107–86 BCE
ROLE	General

Sulla

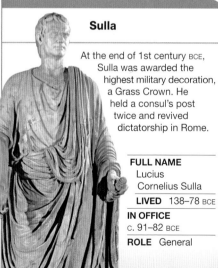

At the end of 1st century BCE, Sulla was awarded the highest military decoration, a Grass Crown. He held a consul's post twice and revived dictatorship in Rome.

FULL NAME	Lucius Cornelius Sulla
LIVED	138–78 BCE
IN OFFICE	c. 91–82 BCE
ROLE	General

Pompey

A popular Roman commander, Pompey adopted the title Magnus ("the great") in honor of his military successes. In 48 BCE, he fled to Egypt after his defeat by Caesar, but was killed on King Ptolemy XIII's orders.

FULL NAME	Gnaeus Pompeius Magnus
LIVED	106–48 BCE
IN OFFICE	52–51 BCE
ROLE	General

Nobles

The nobility in the Roman Empire were people who were in the highest political posts or whose ancestors had held such positions. As part of the upper class in the society, they had special status and privileges, along with influence within the Roman government.

Marcus Furius Camillus

Also known as the second founder of Rome, Camillus is famous for bringing stability after the chaos caused by Gauls' sacking of Rome in 390 BCE. According to historians Plutarch and Livy, he was appointed dictator five times. This Renaissance (a period in history) painting shows him in 15th-century uniform.

FULL NAME	Marcus Furius Camillus
LIVED	446–365 BCE
IN OFFICE	403–365 BCE
TITLE	Dictator

Flag of victory

Lucius Junius Brutus

After winning a revolt against Tarquinius Superbus, the last Roman king, Brutus became the founder of the Roman Republic and one of the first consuls. Experts think that he sentenced his own sons to death when they tried to restore the reign of kings.

FULL NAME	Lucius Junius Brutus
LIVED	Died 509 BCE
IN OFFICE	509 BCE
TITLE	Consul

Marcus Claudius Marcellus

After killing the Gallic military leader Viridomarus at the Battle of Clastidium in 222 BCE, Marcellus was awarded the *spolia opima*, the highest award for Roman generals. During his fifth consulship, he took part in the Second Punic War (218–201 BCE) and was killed in an ambush.

FULL NAME Marcus Claudius Marcellus

LIVED c. 268–208 BCE

IN OFFICE 222–208 BCE

TITLE Consul

Marcellus earned the title "Sword of Rome" because of his triumphs on the battlefield.

Cato the Elder

Cato was notable for his conservative outlook. He wanted to get rid of the Greek influence on Roman life, which he believed was harming traditional Roman principles and discipline.

FULL NAME Marcus Porcius Cato

LIVED 234–149 BCE

IN OFFICE
195–184 BCE

TITLE
Consul, censor

Cato the Younger

Great-grandson of Cato the Elder, Cato the Younger is well known for opposing Julius Caesar and promoting the Republic. He is said to have been extremely truthful and sincere and to have worked honestly in a system that was full of dishonest and unfair people.

FULL NAME Marcus Porcius Cato Uticensis

LIVED 95–46 BCE

IN OFFICE Between 63 and 55 BCE

TITLE Praetor

Marcus Licinius Crassus

Crassus played an important role in the transformation of the Roman Republic into the Roman Empire. He is also famous for being the wealthiest man in ancient Rome. He became more important after defeating the slave leader Spartacus.

FULL NAME Marcus Licinius Crassus

LIVED 115–53 BCE

IN OFFICE 70–53 BCE

TITLE Triumvir

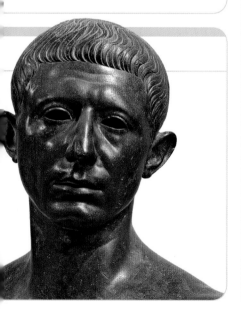

Marcus Junius Brutus

Brutus led a conspiracy to assassinate Julius Caesar. He later killed himself after his troops were defeated by Caesar's grand-nephew and adopted son, Octavian (later known as Augustus). This 16th-century bust was sculpted by Michelangelo.

LIVED 85–42 BCE

IN OFFICE 53 BCE, 44 BCE

TITLE Quaestor, Praetor

Thinkers

The Romans were great achievers and left behind a rich heritage in literature, science, and other fields. Poets, writers, historians, philosophers, and many others had a tremendous influence on the empire's culture and thought.

Ovid

Ovid was one of the greatest and most popular Roman poets. He was exiled to Tomis, Romania, by Emperor Augustus for reasons that are unclear. This statue stands at Sulmona, his birthplace.

LIVED 43 BCE–17 CE

ROLE Poet

FAMOUS FOR Poems *Ars Amatoria* and *Metamorphoses*

Cicero

A popular politician, speaker, and philosopher, Cicero was in favor of the Republic and opposed Caesar's dictatorship. His letters to his friend Atticus tell us about the history of the late Republic. He was later murdered for speaking out against the government.

LIVED 106–43 BCE

ROLE Philosopher, writer

FAMOUS FOR Historical and philosophical writings

Virgil

The son of a farmer, Virgil studied public speaking, medicine, and philosophy in Rome before he began to write poetry. In this Roman mosaic, he is seated between two muses (goddesses of the arts), writing the epic poem *The Aeneid*, which describes the adventures of Aeneas, a Trojan hero.

LIVED 70–19 BCE

ROLE Poet

FAMOUS FOR *The Aeneid* and poems related to country life

Seneca

Poet, philosopher, and lawyer, Seneca belonged to the Stoic school of philosophy, which believed in leading a noble life. Empress Agrippina appointed him to tutor her son, Nero. Seneca was, however, accused of plotting to murder Nero and committed suicide.

LIVED c. 4 BCE–65 CE

ROLE Philosopher

FAMOUS FOR Essays, letters, and tragic plays

Ptolemy

Ptolemy proposed a view of the universe with Earth at the center. Scientists followed his theory for almost 1,400 years. This illustration shows Ptolemy with a quadrant, an astronomical tool.

LIVED c. 85–168 CE

ROLE Astronomer

FAMOUS FOR Geocentric model (Earth at the center of the universe)

Slaves

Slavery was widespread across the Roman Empire. In Italy, slaves formed up to one-third of the population. Senators sometimes owned thousands of slaves. Most slaves were originally prisoners of war or the children of slaves.

Slave waiting on lady

Roles

Slaves performed difficult or dangerous jobs, such as agricultural labor or mining, or acted as domestic servants. Some even became teachers.

Children as slaves

The children of slave women also became slaves. They could be sold to anyone, breaking up the family, and would do light work until they were old enough to perform hard labor.

SIGNS OF SLAVERY

Slaves were often treated cruelly. They could be chained in **manacles**, or even put to death if they misbehaved.

Slaves often had to wear **tesserae**, ceramic or metal tags, which stated their name and who owned them.

Mosaic of child slave working in kitchen

Altar dedicated by freedman to his master

Freedmen

Slaves could be granted freedom by their master, or could buy it if they saved enough money. They then became freedmen, but yet often had to offer services to their former master and live in his household.

Gladiators

The emperor and other Roman officials organized gladiatorial games—combats between professional fighters, sometimes to the death. Mainly chosen from among criminals and prisoners of war, gladiators lived and trained in special schools. Some could earn their freedom by winning enough fights.

The fights

The main gladiatorial games were fights between pairs of men that continued until one gave in or was killed. The games also included animal hunts, often featuring exotic beasts, such as lions or leopards.

Mosaic of gladiator battling leopard

At a show

The games took place in amphitheaters (large oval structures) that could seat up to 50,000 spectators. People of higher social status, such as senators, had places reserved at the front, while women were allowed only in the topmost area.

Trapdoors
Wild animals were held in cages under the arena. When needed for a game, they were moved up through a trapdoor.

Trapdoor with cage

One of the many entrances for the spectators

Emperor's seat
The emperor had a special box to watch the games. From there he declared whether gladiators who accepted defeat should be killed or spared.

Imperial (royal) box

Samnite helmet with high crest

Popular types

There were different types of gladiator. The most common were Samnites (with a large shield, visored helmet, and sword), Thracians (with a curved sword), and *retiarii* (with a trident and net).

The military

Romans believed they were descended from Mars, the god of war. The most powerful military unit of its time, the Roman army conquered vast lands and helped the empire reach a great size. The army fought lots of wars, such as the war with the Dacian people shown in this carving, and fended off many attacks from its neighbors. Once the empire expanded, one of the main tasks of the army was to spread across the Roman territory and control it.

RATION OF FOOD
Roman soldiers received a ration of about 2 lb (1 kg) wheat grains a day. If they were punished, however, they were given barley instead of wheat.

Roman army

Roman citizens who became soldiers were known as legionaries. The Roman army was the most effective in the ancient world. Professional training, high-quality equipment, regular pay, and 25-year-long service created a force that was rarely defeated over a period of 500 years.

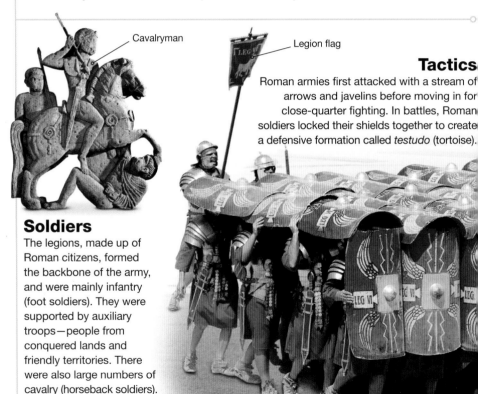

Cavalryman

Legion flag

Tactics

Roman armies first attacked with a stream of arrows and javelins before moving in for close-quarter fighting. In battles, Roman soldiers locked their shields together to create a defensive formation called *testudo* (tortoise).

Soldiers

The legions, made up of Roman citizens, formed the backbone of the army, and were mainly infantry (foot soldiers). They were supported by auxiliary troops—people from conquered lands and friendly territories. There were also large numbers of cavalry (horseback soldiers).

Engineering

Each night on campaign, legionaries built temporary camps. Some of these were later turned into permanent forts made of stone and housed legionary troops, such as the Saalburg fort in Germany shown here.

Testudo formation

UNITS

The army had around 30 legions, each of which included 4,800 soldiers plus 120 cavalry, senior officers, and specialized troops, such as artillery.

One **contubernium** had 10 legionaries

One **centuria** was made up of eight **contubernia**

One **cohort** comprised six **centuriae** (or 48 **contubernia**)

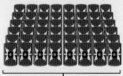

One **legion** consisted of 10 cohorts (or 480 **contubernia**)

 One shield shows one **contubernium** (smallest unit of Roman army)

Weapons

In the early days, men in the Roman army supplied their own weapons. As the empire expanded, the army was reorganized and standard military equipment was produced in a set style. Soldiers had a wide range of weapons, for both long- and short-range attacks.

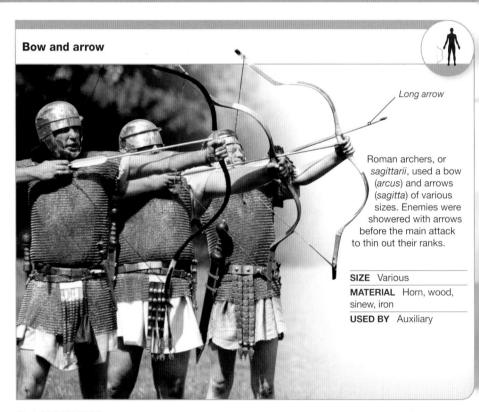

Bow and arrow

Long arrow

Roman archers, or *sagittarii*, used a bow (*arcus*) and arrows (*sagitta*) of various sizes. Enemies were showered with arrows before the main attack to thin out their ranks.

SIZE Various

MATERIAL Horn, wood, sinew, iron

USED BY Auxiliary

Gladius

Most Roman fighting was done at close quarters, the main weapon for which was a short sword called a *gladius*. It was used for stabbing rather than slashing.

SIZE About 20 in (50 cm) long

MATERIAL Iron

USED BY Legionary

Hasta

This heavy thrusting spear called a *hasta* was used in the early Roman period. During the Republican period, only a small section of the army continued to use the *hasta*, since it was replaced by the *pila* and *gladius*.

Wooden shaft

Plumbata

A lead dart, or *plumbata*, was thrown at the enemy from a distance of about 100 ft (30 m). The *plumbatae* were attached to the back of a soldier's shield.

SIZE 6 in (15 cm)

MATERIAL Iron, lead

USED BY Legionary

SIZE About 6½ ft (2 m) long

MATERIAL Wrought iron, wood

USED BY Legionary

Pilum

The throwing javelin, or *pilum*, was hurled at an opponent from around 65 ft (20 m) away. It was designed to bend on impact so that the enemy could not immediately pick it up and reuse it. After the battle, the Romans would gather up the bent javelins, and a blacksmith would straighten them out again.

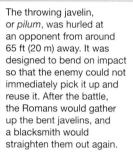

Long iron shank to pierce enemy's shield

SIZE About 6½ ft (2 m) long

MATERIAL Iron, wood

USED BY Legionary

Wooden shaft

Spatha

Cavalry from Celtic tribes (from Europe) introduced the *spatha*, or long sword, to the Romans. It replaced the *gladius*. The *spatha*'s greater length allowed the soldiers to attack with more ease.

Straight double-edged blade

SIZE 2½–3¼ ft (0.75–1 m) long

MATERIAL Iron

USED BY Auxiliary, legionary

Pugio

The Roman dagger, called a *pugio*, had a double-edged blade and was used for stabbing. It was attached to the protective belt worn by the soldiers.

SIZE 8–10 in (20–25 cm)

MATERIAL Iron, bronze

USED BY Legionary

Ballista

The Roman *ballista*, a type of catapult, worked like a large crossbow to shoot arrows or stone balls. Catapults were used to fend off enemy armies and also to attack and conquer towns or forts.

SIZE About 3 ft (1 m) high

MATERIAL Wood, iron

USED BY Legionary

The Roman *ballista* was inspired by the Greek torsion *ballista*, which was developed under Alexander the Great.

Army units had some elements that were unique to them.

▲ The auxiliary cavalry wore face masks like this one at parades.

▲ Each legion had its own *insignia*, or emblem, as depicted on this plate.

▲ The standard bearer held a flag (standard) of the legion called a *vexillum*.

Uniform and armor

As the army grew, Roman soldiers were issued with standard uniforms. Their equipment, especially the armor, gave them an upper hand over their enemies.

Leg guard

Officers wore metal leg protectors, called *greaves* or *ocreae*. These guards covered the leg from knee down. *Greaves* for ceremonial occasions, such as parades, were often highly decorated.

Minerva, goddess of war

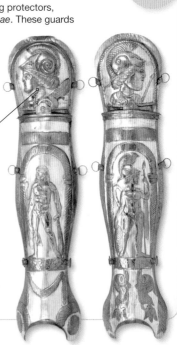

SIZE	16–18 in (40–45 cm)
MATERIAL	Metal, cloth, or leather
USED BY	Centurion

Belt

The *balteus*, or belt, was a soldier's badge of office, worn with a tunic at all times. As soldiers marched, the leather strips made a jangling noise that helped to frighten the enemy.

SIZE Belt size about 47 in (120 cm)

MATERIAL Metal, leather

USED BY Legionary

Heavy pendants weighed down the leather

Coolus

This plain helmet with cheek guards is an example of a Roman *coolus*, which was worn during the late Republican period. The design was inspired by Celtic helmets.

SIZE About 12 in (30 cm)

MATERIAL Brass, bronze

USED BY All soldiers

Metal jacket

Legionary soldiers wore *lorica segmentata*, an armor made of iron and leather strips. It was flexible, allowing for movement, but was so heavy that the soldiers had to help each other put it on and lace it up.

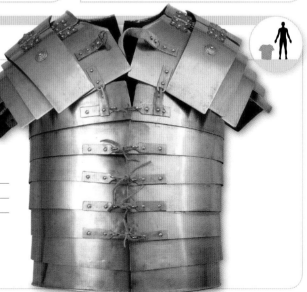

SIZE About 14 in (35 cm)

MATERIAL Iron

USED BY Legionary

Shield

The Roman legionary also carried a *scutum*, a huge wooden shield, for protection. The handle in the middle had a metal cover on the outside, called a boss. This could be used to strike any enemy who got too close.

SIZE	About 40 × 20 in (100 × 50 cm)
MATERIAL	Wood, metal
USED BY	Legionary

Sandals

Military sandals, or *caligae*, were as important as body armor. The soldier's ability to march quickly and over long distances was vital to the army's success. The sandals were strong and well-aired, with patterns of iron hobnails that were specially designed to bear weight and to survive miles of marching.

SIZE	About 9 in (22 cm) long
MATERIAL	Leather, iron
USED BY	Legionary, auxilliary

Straps to tie sandals

Imperial helmet with crest

The Roman Imperial helmet replaced the *coolus* (see p. 49) around the 1st century BCE. Of Gallic (people from Western Europe) origin, this helmet was designed to protect the head, face, and neck without blocking vision or hearing. Centurions (commanders of units called centuries) and other officers wore crests on their helmets, so that their men could see them and follow them in battle.

SIZE About 8 in (20 cm), without crest

MATERIAL Brass, iron

USED BY Ordinary soldiers

Backpack

Each soldier carried a heavy pack—weighing more than 90 lb (40 kg)— over his shoulder. The pack included a tool kit, a dish, and a pan. Legionaries were called "Marius's mules," after the general who started the practice of carrying this backpack.

SIZE Various

MATERIAL Leather

USED BY Legionary

Woolen cloak

Leather bottle for water or wine

Pack for personal items and rations

Marching pole

The Roman navy protected trade ships and kept **pirates at bay**

ROMANS AT SEA
The Roman navy was never as important as the army, although the fleet was expanded during the First Punic War (264–241 BCE). It mainly transported legions on biremes (warships with two decks of oars), as shown in this ancient Roman mosaic, and kept shipments of grain safe from pirates.

Roman wars

From its earliest years, Rome was involved in warfare. At first, Romans fought for control in Italy, and then to gain power over the Mediterranean. Later, Roman armies spread across and battled throughout Europe, North Africa, and the Middle East.

Latin warrior

Early warfare

During the first centuries of its existence, Rome fought wars against other peoples such as the Latins, Etruscans, Volscians, and Samnites. By winning these wars, Rome had conquered all of Italy by 218 BCE.

Figure believed to be Dacian king Decebalus fleeing from the Romans

Expansion

As Rome's territory expanded, more wars broke out against peoples such as the Dacians (of modern Romania), whom it conquered in 101–106 CE. They were also almost in constant warfare against the Parthians and Sassanians of Persia.

Beyond boundaries

Expansion outside Italy made new enemies, such as the North African Carthaginians, whom Rome defeated in three Punic Wars (264–146 BCE). The Palestinian Jews revolted but failed and the Romans captured Jerusalem in 70 CE.

Relief (carving) showing celebration of Jerusalem's destruction

Cavalryman poised to strike with spear

Civil wars

Rome's bloodiest conflicts were civil wars—conflicts among Romans themselves. Civil wars in the 3rd and 4th centuries CE almost destroyed the empire before Constantine I defeated his rivals, including Maxentius at the Battle of Milvian Bridge in 312 CE.

Maxentius's soldiers drowning as the bridge collapses

Wars and battles

Numerous wars and battles helped the city-state of Rome grow into a large, powerful empire. Along with the ambition to expand the frontiers, generals and consuls encouraged attacks for their personal glory. Under the later empire, the Romans found themselves fighting more defensive wars against invading enemies.

Roman–Etruscan Wars

In their early history, the Romans were constantly at war against the Etruscans of northern Italy. This oil painting shows Rome's victory in one such battle in the 7th century BCE. This battle was led by Tullus Hostilius, the third king of Rome, against the Etruscan tribes of Fidenae and Veii.

DATE 753–308 BCE

REGION Etruria, Italy

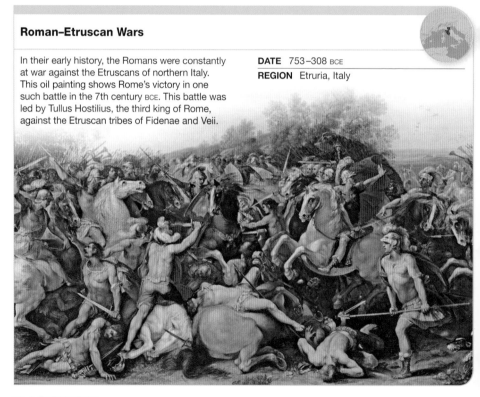

Samnite Wars

The Romans fought three wars against the Samnites—people from Samnium, Italy. Both sides fought hard. Although the Romans suffered a major defeat in 321 BCE during a battle in the Second Samnite War, they won at the end of the wars and established themselves as the supreme power in Italy. This 4th-century BCE tomb painting shows Samnite soldiers.

DATE 343–290 BCE

REGION South Central Italy

Pyrrhic War

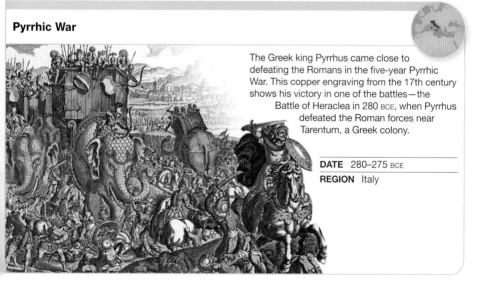

The Greek king Pyrrhus came close to defeating the Romans in the five-year Pyrrhic War. This copper engraving from the 17th century shows his victory in one of the battles—the Battle of Heraclea in 280 BCE, when Pyrrhus defeated the Roman forces near Tarentum, a Greek colony.

DATE 280–275 BCE

REGION Italy

Punic Wars

The First Punic War established Rome as a naval power. This 16th-century image shows Carthaginian general Hannibal leading forces to victory against Rome in a battle during the Second Punic War. In the third and final war, Rome destroyed Carthage.

DATE 264–146 BCE

REGION Western Mediterranean, Italy, and north Africa

Germanic Wars

The series of battles and sieges over several centuries between the Romans and many Germanic tribes is known collectively as the Germanic Wars. This relief (carving) shows the struggle between the two forces. The Germanic tribes became the main enemies of the Western Roman Empire.

DATE 113 BCE–554 CE

REGION Europe

Gallic Wars

This 20th-century painting shows Gallic chieftain Vercingetorix on a horse, surrendering to Julius Caesar after the decisive Battle of Alesia (52 BCE). This Roman victory extended the empire's rule over Gaul and boosted Caesar's political career.

DATE 58–50 BCE

REGION Gaul, Germania (Germany), and Britannia (Britain)

Roman–Persian Wars

Many battles were fought between the Romans and the Persians. Their rivalry of about 700 years ended only with the gradual decline of the two empires. This Persian cameo shows the Persian king Shapur I seizing Emperor Valerian in the Battle of Edessa (260 CE).

DATE 92 BCE–629 CE

REGION West Asia, Eastern Europe, and Egypt

The 2,500 figures carved on Trajan's Column show battles including Emperor Trajan's

victory in the Dacian Wars

TRAJAN'S TRIUMPH
The Dacians lived in an area north of the Roman Empire by the Danube River. After Trajan defeated them in the Dacian Wars (101–106 CE) and brought Dacia under Roman rule, he declared more than 100 days of celebrations. Some historians say the Romans claimed 365,000 lb (165,500 kg) of gold from the treasure of Dacian king Decebalus.

Enemies

From a small city on the banks of the Tiber River in Italy, Rome grew to command a vast and powerful empire. Its incredible wealth, prosperity, and power made it plenty of enemies. With the empire expanding, its enemies had to defend their own borders, but over time, they were able to launch attacks on the empire.

Hamilcar Barca

During the final phase of the First Punic War (264–241 BCE), Hamilcar Barca led the Carthaginian forces in Sicily, where Rome and Carthage fought for control. Barca occupied Mt. Ercte and later Mt. Eryx, despite determined efforts by the Roman army to remove him.

LIVED 275–228 BCE

REGION Carthage, Tunisia

Hannibal

In 218 BCE, Hamilcar Barca's son marched into Roman territory, crossing the Alps with 100,000 men and 40 elephants. He inflicted huge defeats on the Romans but could not take Rome. This commander is known for his battle plans and has been given the title "father of strategy."

LIVED 247–183 BCE

REGION Carthage, Tunisia

18th-century statue of Hannibal

Mithridates VI

An ambitious general, Mithridates was the king of Pontus and Armenia Minor in northern Anatolia (Turkey). He engaged Rome in three wars known as the Mithridatic Wars (88–63 BCE). He fought with many great Roman generals, such as Sulla, Lucullus, and Pompey.

LIVED 132–63 BCE

REGION
Anatolia, Turkey

Cleopatra VII

By joining forces with Julius Caesar and Mark Antony, the last Egyptian Queen, Cleopatra, hoped to gain power over Rome. After Caesar's murder and Antony's death, she killed herself by letting a snake bite her.

LIVED 69–30 BCE

REGION Egypt

Vercingetorix

Vercingetorix was the chief of the Arverni (from Auvergne, France) and led a group of tribes against Julius Caesar's forces. He inflicted extensive damage on the Roman army, but was defeated in the Battle of Alesia (52 BCE). This 19th-century statue was erected at the battle site.

LIVED 82–46 BCE

REGION
Auvergne, France

Arminius

A leader of the Germanic Cherusci tribe, Arminius defeated three Roman legions at the Battle of the Teutoburg Forest in 9 CE. His victory changed the course of history, because the Romans made no more attempts to occupy Germania between the Rhine and Elbe rivers. This statue was erected on the 2,000th anniversary of the battle.

LIVED	18 BCE–21 CE
REGION	Germany

Boudica

Boudica's husband, Prasutagus, was an ally of Rome and ruled the Iceni (a Celtic tribe in Roman Britain) free of any Roman control. After his death, the Romans stole his lands. Angered by this, Boudica attacked and destroyed a Roman legion and burned down several Roman cities. This 19th-century statue stands in her honor in London, England.

LIVED Died 61 CE
REGION East Anglia, Britain

Boudica became a legend in Britain and Queen Victoria was often compared to her.

Zenobia

Queen of Palmyra, in Syria, Zenobia conquered Egypt (then ruled by the Romans). Her exploits in Syria, Lebanon, and Palestine forced Emperor Aurelian to shift his attention to her territories. She was taken hostage, and this 19th-century statue shows her in chains.

LIVED 240–274 CE
REGION Palmyra, Syria

Alaric

Alaric, shown in this 19th-century portrait, was the ruler of the Goths (a nomadic tribe of Germans). He is famous for his siege of Rome, also known as the Sack of Rome, in 410 CE. The empire could not completely recover from this defeat and its decline began from here.

LIVED
370–410 CE
REGION The Balkan Peninsula

Religion

Ancient Romans believed that gods and spirits controlled everything in their lives, so prayer was very important to them. People worshiped at altars in their homes, the army had religious customs, and emperors, too, performed religious rituals. Priests most often came from higher classes, and usually were ones who held political positions. This 2nd-century CE mosaic shows goddess Diana in a hunting scene.

CHARON
The Romans borrowed the idea of the Greek god Charon ferrying the dead to the underwold. Often, slaves dressed as Charon at funerals.

Religious beliefs

Roman religion was extremely varied. The Romans worshiped the greatest of the gods Jupiter, Juno, and Minerva (known as the Capitoline Triad) as well as many lesser and traditional deities. Fifteen priests, known as *flamines*, served the main gods and supervised their festivals.

"Horn of plenty," a symbol of nourishment

In the house

At home, the Romans worshiped gods called Lares and Penates. Almost every household had an altar for them. There were other lesser, but popular gods, including Ceres and Vesta.

Worshiper leads sheep to be sacrificed

Bronze statue of one of the Lares

Sacrifice

Animal sacrifice on a public altar in front of the gods' temples was an important religious ritual. An especially elaborate sacrifice was the *suovetaurilia*, involving a sheep, a pig, and a bull.

Cults

The most widespread cults—religious groups devoted to a particular idea or god—in Roman society were of Isis, an Egyptian goddess, and Mithras, an eastern god. These cults had special priests and were popular in the army.

Painting showing priests of Isis performing ritual

Rise of Christianity

In the 1st century CE, Christianity, with its belief in one god, was introduced in Rome. For centuries, it was practiced in secret and Christians were persecuted. Only when Emperor Constantine legalized it in 313 CE could Christians openly build churches.

Gods

The ancient Romans worshiped lots of deities and spirits. They adopted some Greek gods and Romanized them, and they combined others with their existing gods. As the empire expanded, they absorbed gods from many other civilizations.

Jupiter

In Roman mythology, Jupiter was regarded as the king of gods. He was the ruler of the heavens, and his weapon was a thunderbolt, which he would hurl when angry. An eagle carried this bolt in its claws. Jupiter was often represented on Roman coins.

ALTERNATIVE NAMES Zeus, Jove

RELATED SYMBOL Thunderbolt

Juno

The goddess of marriage and childbirth, Juno (Jupiter's wife) was worshiped mainly by Roman women, who celebrated her festival, the Matronalia, on March 1 every year. She was also the patron goddess of Rome.

ALTERNATIVE NAME Hera

RELATED SYMBOL Peacock

Juno was usually depicted wearing a goatskin cloak

Neptune

Neptune ruled the oceans and seas, and his trident (three-pointed spear) symbolized his control over water. In another role, he is hailed as the god of horse racing and said to be the creator of horses.

ALTERNATIVE NAME Poseidon

RELATED SYMBOL Trident

Minerva

In art, Minerva, the goddess of war, is usually shown clad in armor. In this stone cameo (a form of carving), she is wearing a helmet. Minerva was also the goddess of arts and crafts and is said to have invented the flute.

ALTERNATIVE NAME Athena

RELATED SYMBOL Owl

Mars

The most respected god on the battlefield, Mars, the god of war, rode a chariot drawn by four fire-breathing horses. His priests, who were called the *Salii*, dressed in war clothes and carried swords.

ALTERNATIVE NAME Ares

RELATED SYMBOL Vulture

Venus

The goddess of love and beauty, Venus was born at sea and floated to the shore on a scallop shell. Later, she married the god Vulcan, who made her a golden carriage drawn by doves.

ALTERNATIVE NAME Aphrodite

RELATED SYMBOL Dove

Apollo

The Sun god, Apollo, was thought to be a healer, because the Sun's warmth was associated with general well-being. Apollo also played the lyre and was the god of music and poetry.

ALTERNATIVE NAME Phoebus Apollo

RELATED SYMBOL Lyre

Diana

Apollo's twin sister, Diana was the goddess of the Moon and of hunting: some myths say the god Pan gave her hunting dogs. During her festival Nemoralia, however, people were not allowed to hunt and kill animals.

ALTERNATIVE NAME Artemis

RELATED SYMBOLS Bow and arrow

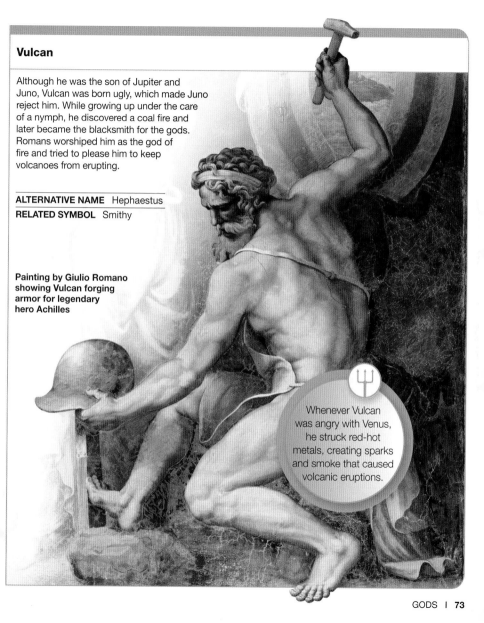

Vulcan

Although he was the son of Jupiter and Juno, Vulcan was born ugly, which made Juno reject him. While growing up under the care of a nymph, he discovered a coal fire and later became the blacksmith for the gods. Romans worshiped him as the god of fire and tried to please him to keep volcanoes from erupting.

ALTERNATIVE NAME Hephaestus
RELATED SYMBOL Smithy

Painting by Giulio Romano showing Vulcan forging armor for legendary hero Achilles

Whenever Vulcan was angry with Venus, he struck red-hot metals, creating sparks and smoke that caused volcanic eruptions.

Bacchus

The god of wine was associated with enjoyment, and his festivals, Bacchanalia, were a time for wild parties and wine drinking. Bacchus was accompanied by female followers and carried a *thyrsus*, a staff of giant fennel.

ALTERNATIVE NAME Dionysus

RELATED SYMBOL Grapevine

The rituals in honor of Bacchus got so wild and unmanageable that the Senate banned them from 186 BCE.

Ceres

Ceres was the goddess of agriculture. It was said that she taught people to plow, sow, and reap. According to myth, if Ceres was angry, the crops would die, and so the gods and people tried to keep her happy.

ALTERNATIVE NAME Demeter
RELATED SYMBOL Poppy

Growing plants around Ceres on 3rd-century CE mosaic

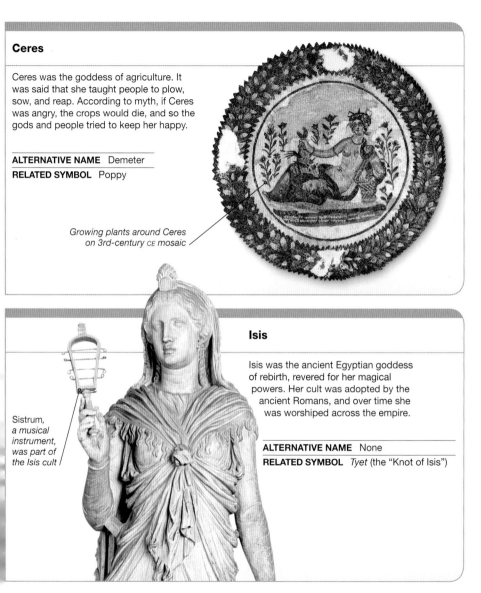

Isis

Isis was the ancient Egyptian goddess of rebirth, revered for her magical powers. Her cult was adopted by the ancient Romans, and over time she was worshiped across the empire.

ALTERNATIVE NAME None
RELATED SYMBOL *Tyet* (the "Knot of Isis")

Sistrum, a musical instrument, was part of the Isis cult

Flora

The goddess of flowers, Flora was associated with spring and the renewal of life, and often shown in art as wearing a crown of flowers. She was also linked with Fauna, the goddess of animals.

ALTERNATIVE NAME None
RELATED SYMBOL Flowers

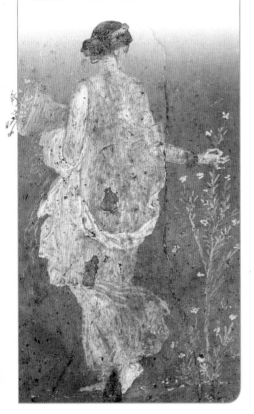

Mercury

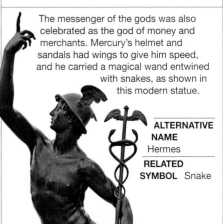

The messenger of the gods was also celebrated as the god of money and merchants. Mercury's helmet and sandals had wings to give him speed, and he carried a magical wand entwined with snakes, as shown in this modern statue.

ALTERNATIVE NAME Hermes
RELATED SYMBOL Snake

Mithras

The cult of Mithras was brought to ancient Rome from India and Persia. It was especially popular with the empire's soldiers. In Roman religion, Mithras was the god of the Sun. He killed a bull, whose blood soaked and fertilized the soil.

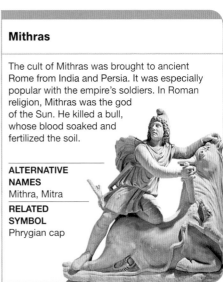

ALTERNATIVE NAMES Mithra, Mitra
RELATED SYMBOL Phrygian cap

Saturn

Legend says that Saturn, the god of sowing, was exiled by his son, Jupiter, because he was cruel to his children. After being overthrown, Saturn left Olympus and settled in Italy. There he lived peacefully and taught his people agriculture.

ALTERNATIVE NAME Kronos

RELATED SYMBOL Scythe

To join the Mithras cult, Romans had to take part in a ritual in which they were

blindfolded

and given passwords

CULT OF MITHRAS
Many Romans were part of a religious cult dedicated to Mithras. The cult practiced rituals, but most of these were kept highly secret during the time, and its members had to swear an oath that they would keep its rites and traditions hidden. One of the central images in Mithraic temples was Mithras slaying a bull. He was usually shown accompanied by animals, such as a snake and a dog, reaching up for the bull's blood.

Buildings and monuments

The Romans were great architects and builders. They constructed grand temples, palatial buildings, bridges that lasted for centuries, and much more. Useful structures, such as aqueducts (to supply water), helped the cities to survive. This ancient temple shows one of the Roman innovations in construction—the arch.

FOUNTAINS
Fountains, such as this one in Pompeii, were built in city streets. Engineers used the pressure from water falling from a height to make it jet into the air.

Cities

The Roman civilization was centered mainly around towns and cities. From Rome itself, with more than a million inhabitants, to tiny settlements in northern Britain, towns and cities throughout the empire shared many similar features.

City plan

Roman cities were generally arranged in a square grid pattern. Their focal point was the forum, a central open space around with law courts and Senate House grouped around. Nearby were the temples of the main gods and central markets. Most Roman cities also had public bathhouses and amphitheaters for entertainment.

The city of Rome (left)
1. Tiber River
2. Temple of Jupiter
3. The Forum
4. Trajan's Market
5. Colosseum
6. Temple of Claudius

TIBER RIVER

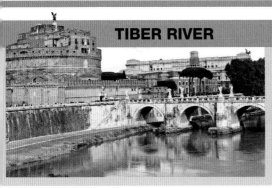

Rome developed around the Tiber. This river divided Rome's main quarters to the east from the more newly developed areas to the west. It provided a crucial river route to Rome's main port at Ostia, 16 miles (25 km) downriver.

Provincial cities

The rich people of cities across the empire, such as Volubilis in Mauretania (modern Morocco), gave money to adorn their home towns with buildings that mirrored Rome. Volubilis had urban villas, bathhouses, triumphal arches, a forum, and a basilica (public building), all arranged around the city's main east-west highway.

Ruins of the basilica, Volubilis, Morocco

The oasis city of Palmyra was so prosperous that it was called the

Bride of the Desert

TRADING POST
Palmyra, established around 2000 BCE, was a fertile oasis in the middle of the Syrian desert. It was a vital stop for traders traveling long distances in caravans (a large group of people, animals, and vehicles), and the city's importance grew when it became part of the Roman Empire in the 1st century CE.

Architecture

The Romans were skilled architects and engineers, erecting monumental public buildings throughout the empire. Their mastery of techniques such as the arch and the use of concrete enabled their buildings to stand for centuries.

Thinner concrete used higher up the dome

Tympanum, or triangular pediment

Frieze

Columns on a raised podium

Greek influence

Early Roman architecture was influenced by ancient Greece. This typical Greek temple in Sicily shows features later used in many Roman buildings, such as columns, *tympana*, and friezes (horizontal sculpted bands).

Domes

Using their knowledge of concrete, the Romans constructed huge domes, such as the Pantheon's, which is 139 ft (42.3 m) across. They used arches to spread the massive weight of the domes.

Pantheon temple, Rome

Arches

The arch is a common feature in Roman architecture. The rounded arches of the Romans differ from the pointed style of arches made by Arabs or in late medieval period in Europe.

Ruins of Leptis Magna (in modern Libya)

BUILDING TOOLS

A bronze triangle was used for measuring right angles, with an instrument called a plumb line to check vertical alignment.

A leveling staff with adjustable disk was used to check differences in height.

Homes

Roman houses varied from grand city mansions to large country villas, and even *insulae*—apartment buildings where the urban poor lived. Houses of the rich were mostly of brick, with two floors, built around a central *atrium* or reception courtyard.

Roman house

The *atrium* was the most public space in the house. The private rooms, such as bedrooms, were built around the *peristylium*, a second open place. The dining room, or *triclinium*, might be near either of these.

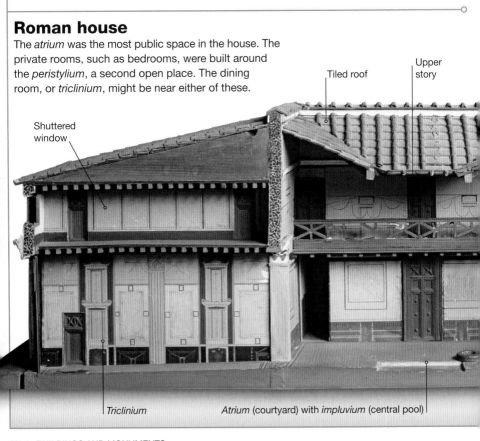

Tiled roof

Upper story

Shuttered window

Triclinium

Atrium (courtyard) with *impluvium* (central pool)

TYPES

Villas These were luxurious country houses, built by wealthy Romans. This one is in Pompeii.

Domus This house in Ostia Antica, the port of Rome, is typical of the urban dwellings, or *domus*, of the wealthy.

Insulae Apartment blocks, such as this reconstructed *insula* in Herculaneum, were vulnerable to catastrophic fires.

Outside wall

Cubiculum (bedroom)

Peristylium (garden)

Temples

Roman towns had lots of temples, usually built in important locations, such as forums, or on major roads. Each temple was dedicated to a specific god, whose statue was housed in a central room called a *cella*.

FOCUS ON...
BUILDING MATERIALS
The Romans used different materials for construction.

Temple of Jupiter
Pompeii, Italy

Like many other Roman cities, Pompeii had a temple dedicated to Jupiter, who was considered to be the supreme god. Sacrificial offerings and city treasures were stored in a chamber below the temple's main hall.

BUILT IN Mid-2nd century BCE

BUILT BY Unknown

LOCATION Pompeii, Italy

Temple of Bacchus
Baalbek, Lebanon

The Temple of Bacchus in Baalbek is one of the best-preserved ancient temples in the world. The worship of Bacchus, the god of wine, was often followed by wild, drunken festivals. People performed theater as part of these festive celebrations.

BUILT IN c. 150 CE

BUILT BY Antoninus Pius

LOCATION Baalbek, Lebanon

▲ Concrete was used extensively to build massive structures, such as the dome of the Pantheon.

▲ Marble was used mainly for decoration. Relief work, a type of carving, on marble was used on many structures.

▲ Furnaces were built to bake clay bricks. Both public and private buildings were constructed with bricks.

Pantheon
Rome, Italy

A temple devoted to all of the gods worshiped in ancient Rome, the Pantheon was built by Marcus Agrippa during the reign of Augustus. It was later rebuilt by Hadrian and was the world's largest domed structure until the 15th century.

BUILT IN 126 CE

BUILT BY Hadrian

LOCATION Rome, Italy

Maison Carrée
Nîmes, France

In ancient Rome, godlike status was often given to emperors and their relatives, along with governors, too. The Maison Carrée was dedicated to Gaius and Lucius Caesar, the adopted sons of Emperor Augustus.

BUILT IN c. 16 BCE	
BUILT BY Agrippa	
LOCATION Nîmes, France	

Temple of Bel
Palmyra, Syria

The Temple of Bel was built upon the remains of a temple that dated back to the ancient Greek civilization. This temple stands out as one of the largest and most prominent among other ancient structures in the prosperous city of Palmyra.

This temple was turned into a church near the end of Roman era and later, into a fort.

BUILT IN 1st–2nd century CE
BUILT BY Unknown
LOCATION Palmyra, Syria

Temple of Jupiter
Sbeitla, Tunisia

The Temple of Jupiter is one of the most impressive remains of the ancient Roman city of Sufetula, in Tunisia. This temple is next to those of two other important Roman gods—Juno and Minerva.

BUILT IN 1st–2nd century CE
BUILT BY Antoninus Pius
LOCATION Sbeitla, Tunisia

Garni Temple
Kotayk, Armenia

Dedicated to Mithras, this temple was built by the Armenian king Tiridates I when Armenia was at peace with Rome. This Greco-Roman (a style inspired by ancient Greeks and Romans) temple was made of basalt.

BUILT IN 1st century CE
BUILT BY Tiridates I
LOCATION Kotayk, Armenia

Temple of Augustus and Livia
Vienne, France

This temple is one of the two main ancient Roman structures that have survived in Vienne. Initially, this temple was dedicated only to Augustus Caesar. In 41 CE, it was dedicated to his wife, Livia, as well.

BUILT IN	20–10 BCE
BUILT BY	Claudius
LOCATION	Vienne, France

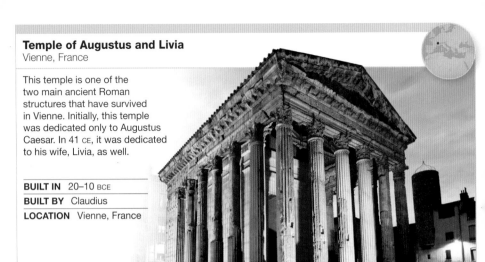

Temple of Venus and Roma
Rome, Italy

Emperor Hadrian himself played an important role in planning the design of this temple. It was later renovated by Emperor Maxentius after most of it was damaged in a fire. Now, the Santa Francesca Romana church stands at the site of the ruins of this temple.

BUILT IN	135 CE
BUILT BY	Hadrian
LOCATION	Rome, Italy

Church

Remains of chamber that contained the figure of Venus

Temple of Zeus
Aizanoi, Turkey

This temple honoring Zeus is one
of the best-preserved temples in Anatolia.
Sixteen of its original 17 pillars are still standing.
The magnificent statue of Zeus in its inner
sanctum was lost long ago.

BUILT IN
2nd century CE
BUILT BY
Hadrian
LOCATION
Aizanoi,
Anatolia, Turkey

Temple of Venus Genetrix
Rome, Italy

Julius Caesar dedicated this temple
to Venus Genetrix—the goddess of motherhood
and domesticity. Its treasures included a statue
of Venus, and one of Caesar and Cleopatra.

BUILT IN 46 BCE
BUILT BY Julius Caesar
LOCATION Rome, Italy

*Columns that
surrounded the
original temple*

PANTHEON'S DOME

The oculus—a round opening at the top of a dome—was first used by the Romans. The Pantheon's oculus lets sunlight stream in. It is the only source of natural light in the temple. On a few special days each year, a single sunbeam comes through the oculus and falls perfectly on the doorway to light it up.

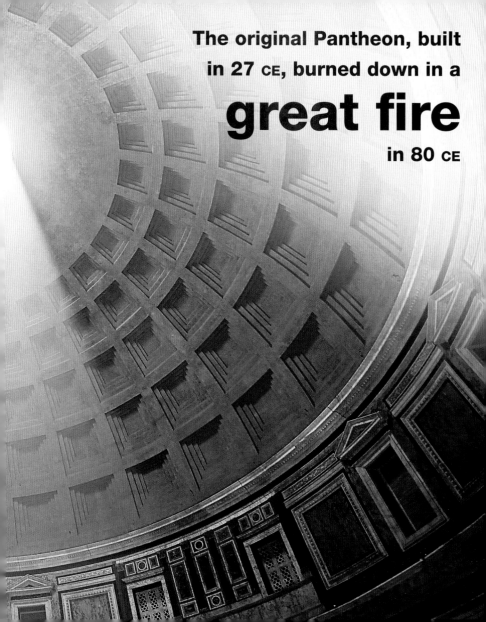

The original Pantheon, built in 27 CE, burned down in a **great fire** in 80 CE

Villas and palaces

A Roman villa was not simply a place to live; it was also a symbol of the owner's position and wealth. Wealthy Romans often had a villa in the country (in addition to a house in town), sometimes building estates with more than one villa. They decorated the interiors with mosaics, frescoes, and fine furniture.

Hadrian's Villa
Tivoli, Italy

Hadrian's Villa was built purely as a luxury retreat, and it had no working farms attached, which was not the usual practice. The estate had buildings inspired by Hadrian's favourite sights from his travels around Greece and Egypt, including a pool he had seen in Alexandria.

BUILT IN   118–134 CE

BUILT BY   Hadrian

LOCATION   Tivoli, Italy

Villa of the Mysteries
Pompeii, Italy

Outside the main town of Pompeii lies the Villa of Mysteries, with its well-preserved, colorful frescoes. Most of these frescoes depict religious rites and ceremonies.

BUILT IN   c. 1st century CE

BUILT BY   Unknown, possibly Livia

LOCATION   Pompeii, Italy

Villa Romana del Casale
Sicily, Italy

This villa is famous for housing the largest collection of surviving Roman mosaics. It was in use even after the empire fell, but was destroyed in a landslide in the 12th century CE. Its original owner is thought to be a senator or a member of the imperial family.

BUILT IN   4th century CE

BUILT BY   Unknown

LOCATION   Sicily, Italy

Diocletian's Palace
Split, Croatia

Diocletian had this palace built as his retirement home. After the fall of the empire, locals made their homes, stores, and restaurants in the palace complex. Diocletian's mausoleum has been converted into a cathedral.

BUILT IN   4th century CE

BUILT BY   Diocletian

LOCATION   Split, Croatia

Baths

Large public baths were popular meeting places among Romans. Men and women used the baths at different times of day, enjoying the hot and cold pools, steam rooms, and exercise rooms.

▲ Romans used olive oil, stored in flasks, to rub on their bodies. There was no soap in ancient Rome.

▲ Strigil, a curved metal blade, was used to scrape off the oil and dirt.

The Great Bath
Bath, England

The Romans built the Great Bath around the natural hot spring at Aquae Sulis, now known as Bath. It contained a shrine to the goddess Sulis, whom the Romans worshiped as Minerva. Surrounded by villas, it was a place to relax.

BUILT IN	1st–2nd century CE
BUILT BY	Claudius
LOCATION	Bath, England

Forum Baths
Pompeii, Italy

The Forum Baths were the smallest of the Pompeii baths. They were the only working baths in Pompeii after a major earthquake in 62 CE.

BUILT IN   1st century BCE

BUILT BY   Sulla

LOCATION   Pompeii, Italy

Imperial Baths
Trier, Germany

Aside from those in Rome, the Imperial Baths are the largest surviving Roman baths. After 360 CE, their use was discontinued, and later Roman emperors turned them into barracks.

BUILT IN   4th century CE

BUILT BY   Constantius Chlorus

LOCATION   Trier, Germany

Baths of Trajan
Rome, Italy

This massive complex was built by Trajan at the site of the ruined palace of Emperor Nero. Its underground tank, known as Sette Sale or Seven Halls, can store up to 2.1 million gallons (8 million liters) of water.

BUILT IN   104–109 CE

BUILT BY   Trajan

LOCATION   Rome, Italy

Open-air arenas

The Romans enjoyed theatrical shows, chariot racing, and blood sports, such as gladiatorial fights between men and animals. Crowds gathered in specially built venues, such as amphitheaters, to watch these.

FOCUS ON...
VENUES
Arenas differed in structure according to their purpose.

Theater of Aphrodisias
Karacasu, Turkey

Originally built by the ancient Greeks, this theater contains a large collection of Greek and Roman artifacts. When it was being repaired, Zoilos, a slave freed by Emperor Octavian, dedicated the theater to the goddess Aphrodite and the Roman people.

BUILT IN	3rd century BCE–2nd century CE
BUILT BY	Ancient Greeks
LOCATION	Near Karacasu, Turkey

Colosseum
Rome, Italy

The spoils of the Jewish–Roman Wars (66–73 CE) were used to build the Colosseum—the largest amphitheater of ancient Rome. Spectators entered through numbered gates to watch gladiator fights and other sports, but the emperor had a private entrance under the seats.

▲ Circuses, such as the Circus Maximus, were U-shaped and long, with seats on three sides; they were used for chariot races.

▲ Theaters for plays were semicircular, with the stage on one side and tiered seats along the semicircle.

▲ The audience could sit all around the circular or oval arenas called amphitheaters, which hosted many events.

BUILT IN 70–80 CE

BUILT BY Vespasian and Titus

LOCATION Rome, Italy

Amphitheater of El Jem
El Jem, Tunisia

Located in a village in Tunisia, this amphitheater could hold up to 35,000 spectators. It was made completely of stone, and its size and construction are often compared to those of the Colosseum.

BUILT IN 238 CE

BUILT BY Gordian

LOCATION El Jem, Tunisia

Pompeii Amphitheater
Pompeii, Italy

This was the first Roman amphitheater made of stone instead of wood. Locals and people from nearby towns would gather to watch the games at this arena. Following a fight between spectators from Pompeii and Nuceria in 59 CE, Emperor Nero shut it for 10 years.

BUILT IN	c. 70 BCE
BUILT BY	Quinctius Valgus, Marcius Porcius
LOCATION	Pompeii, Italy

Leptis Magna Theater
Leptis Magna, Libya

The poorer class was only allowed on the top tiers of the theaters. In the Leptis Magna Theater, a colonnaded walk was built to offer them some shade.

Pula Arena
Pula, Croatia

Constructed with local limestone, this amphitheater could seat around 20,000 people. It had two reservoirs containing perfumed water, which was supplied to a fountain and was also sprinkled on the audience.

BUILT IN	27 BCE–81 CE
BUILT BY	Augustus, Claudius, Vespasian, Titus
LOCATION	Pula, Croatia

BUILT IN Completed 1–2 CE
BUILT BY Annobal Tapapius Rufus
LOCATION Leptis Magna, near Khoms, Libya

Uthina Amphitheater
Uthina, Tunisia

Four main entrances led into the Uthina Amphitheater, which was built in a natural depression in a hilly region, with its seats rising on the slopes.

BUILT IN c. 117–138 CE
BUILT BY Hadrian
LOCATION Uthina, Tunisia

Arena of Nîmes
Nîmes, France

The Arena of Nîmes was designed in such a way that a huge canvas could cover it to protect the spectators from sun and rain. It was later turned into a fort by Visigoths, a Germanic tribe. Today, it hosts bullfights.

BUILT IN 70 CE
BUILT BY Vespasian
LOCATION Nîmes, France

THE COLOSSEUM
There were about 80 entrances to the Colosseum and the amphitheater could seat around 50,000 people. The entrances were numbered and spectators were given broken pieces of pottery as "tickets." Each ticket had a number that corresponded to a particular number on an entrance.

The opening games at the Colosseum, which went on for more than 100 days, saw

9,000 animals slaughtered

FOCUS ON...
BRIDGES
Romans were the first to use arches to build bridges.

▲ Fabricius's Bridge, in Rome, built in 62 BCE to replace a burnt wooden one, is still in use today.

▲ Alcántara Bridge in Spain includes the Arch of Triumph, which has many carved tablets on it.

▲ The Pont Julien bridge in France was used for about 2,000 years (until 2005).

Aqueducts

Romans built many aqueducts to carry water. These were bridges, built on arches, with stone channels to supply water to towns. The aqueducts sourced water from distant rivers and lakes and carried it across difficult landscapes.

Aqueduct of Segovia
Segovia, Spain

With 167 arches made of strong granite blocks, the Aqueduct of Segovia was so well built that it was still in use until the 20th century. It is the best preserved of all the Roman aqueducts.

BUILT IN	1st century CE
BUILT BY	Domitian
LOCATION	Segovia, Spain

Park of the Aqueducts
Rome, Italy

A network of 11 aqueducts, now known as the Park of the Aqueducts, was built to meet the water demands of the city of Rome. The system sourced water from as far as 57 miles (92 km).

BUILT IN	312 BCE–226 CE
BUILT BY	Unknown
LOCATION	Rome, Italy

Pont du Gard
Nîmes, France

The three-level Pont du Gard brought water to Nesausas (modern-day Nîmes) from the springs of Uzès. The stone building blocks were so well crafted from stone that the Romans had no need for mortar to bind them together.

BUILT IN	1st century CE
BUILT BY	Agrippa
LOCATION	Nîmes, France

Les Ferreres Aqueduct
Tarragona, Spain

Originally 15 miles (25 km) in length, Les Ferreres carried freshwater from the Francolí River. It is also known as the Devil's Bridge because legends say that the Devil built it.

BUILT IN 1st century BCE– 1st century CE

BUILT BY Augustus

LOCATION Tarragona, Spain

Valens Aqueduct
Istanbul, Turkey

Still in partial use until the 18th century, the Valens Aqueduct was one of the main water sources for Constantinople (now Istanbul). Around 3,021 ft (921 m) of the bridge survives.

BUILT IN 4th century CE

BUILT BY Valens

LOCATION Istanbul, Turkey

Aqueduct of the Miracles
Mérida, Spain

The Aqueduct of the Miracles was made with a combination of stone and brick. It is the largest and the best preserved of the three aqueducts built to supply water to Emerita Augusta (now Mérida).

BUILT IN 1st century CE
BUILT BY Augustus
LOCATION Mérida, Spain

Roman life

The lives of most ancient Romans revolved around cities. People were involved in a variety of work and they had busy social lives, enjoying a variety of shows and celebrating festivals throughout the year. Country life was quieter, with farming as the main occupation. Rich people from cities often went to the countryside to hunt, fish, and relax in their villas. This carving shows a peaceful pastoral (country) scene.

LANGUAGE
The official language across the Roman Empire was Latin. Many modern languages and their alphabets have developed from Latin.

Daily life

Men were actively involved in public life outside the home, but women and children spent most of their time indoors. While women mainly cooked and did housework, children spent their time playing and learning.

Children

Lives of children from rich and poor families were very different. Poorer children had to work to help their families. Richer Roman children started their education with tutors at home. Some boys went to formal schools after they turned 11.

Fresco of a woman

Women

Roman women married young, at around the age of 12, and generally did not work outside the home. Although they did not have the right to vote, they could own property.

Roman relief showing a schoolroom

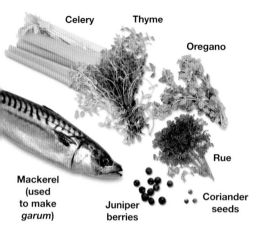

Celery Thyme

Oregano

Rue

Mackerel
(used
to make
garum)

Juniper
berries

Coriander
seeds

Food

Romans kept breakfast (*jentaculum*) and lunch light before the main meal (*cena*) in late afternoon. For rich Romans, this had many courses of meat, fish, and vegetables cooked with herbs. Sauces, including *garum* (fish sauce), were popular and one exotic dish was baked, stuffed dormice.

Country life

Many senators had large estates and villas in the countryside where they spent the summer months because Romans saw country life as an ideal. They knew of different farming methods. This mosaic shows farmers threshing wheat with the help of horses and cattle.

At work

Professionals, businessmen, craftsmen, and laborers made life in cities and the running of country estates possible. Senators and landowners did not generally work. There was a system in which wealthier Romans helped "clients" in many ways, such as to get jobs. In return, clients provided services.

Baker

Romans normally bought bread from bakeries, rather than making it at home. Under the early empire, 200,000 people received the *annona*, a ration of free bread for poorer citizens.

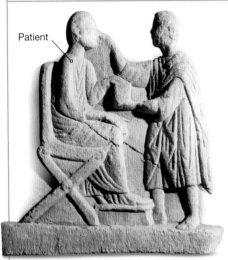

Patient

Roman relief showing an eye doctor

Fresco showing bread distribution

Doctor

Roman doctors were often slaves. Their knowledge of the treatment of diseases was limited. Roman surgery was more advanced, especially in the army, which had specialized hospitals.

Reconstructed Gallo-Roman harvester

Harvesting

Farm workers, who were often slaves, harvested laboriously by hand. Only in the later Roman Empire were automatic harvesting machines introduced, mostly in Gaul (modern-day France).

Storekeepers

Roman merchants often had their stores on the ground floor of their houses. Roman taverns (*thermopolia*) served wine, and some served hot food to their customers.

Model reconstruction of Roman wine shop

Wine was **mixed with water** before serving

Writing

The Romans introduced writing to northern Europe. A form of their alphabet is still used today, with four additional letters—J, U, W, and Y—added to the 22 they used. The Romans wrote on many materials, with inscriptions carved in stone, trade accounts on broken pots, poems on papyrus, and personal letters scratched on wax tablets.

Inkwell

Romans used different types of inkwell to store their writing ink, or *atramentum librarium*. This one from the reign of Emperor Nero is fashioned with horizontal ridges.

SIZE About 2 × 1¼ in (5 × 3 cm)

MATERIAL Bronze

Papyrus

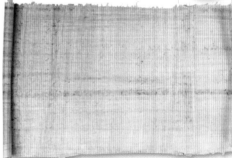

Generally, words were written on reusable wax tablets or thin sheets of wood. Strips of the papyrus plant were also cut, arranged, dried, and then polished to make papyrus sheets or scrolls.

SIZE (Standard) 18½ × 9 in (47 × 22 cm)

MATERIAL Papyrus

Bronze legal document

While the Romans usually wrote on papyrus sheets, stone, or wax tablets, they only used bronze tablets for legal records. Laws and international treaties were also engraved on bronze.

SIZE 5½ × 9 in
(14 × 22 cm)

MATERIAL Bronze

2nd-century CE document declaring the freedom of slaves in Hasta (Spain)

Reed pen

Romans used reed pens dipped in ink to write on papyrus sheets or thin wooden tablets, such as the ones found in Vindolanda, near Hadrian's Wall in northern Britain.

SIZE About 4¾ in (12 cm)

MATERIAL Reed

1st-century CE reed pen from Egypt

Stylus

The pointed end of a bronze stylus (a type of pen) was used to scratch letters on wax tablets. The flat end was used to erase the etchings by smoothing the wax. The three styli shown here date from the 2nd century CE.

SIZE About 6 in (15 cm)

MATERIAL Bronze

In the house

Wealthy Romans lived in luxurious houses with little furniture because they liked space and airy rooms. The lack of clutter also made statues, frescoes, and mosaics stand out. The rich had a lot of luxuries, such as a direct water supply and kitchens—both facilities that the poor did not have in their homes.

Couch and stool

One of the most important pieces of furniture was the couch, on which the Romans laid back and relaxed. They would also recline to dine, drink, and talk. Sometimes couches were high and had to be reached using a little stool. At dinner parties, three people could sit side by side on the couch.

SIZE	(Couch) 29½ × 45 in (74.9 × 114.3 cm) (Stool) 9 x 26½ in (23 x 67 cm)
MATERIAL	Wood, glass, bone
DATE	1st–2nd century CE

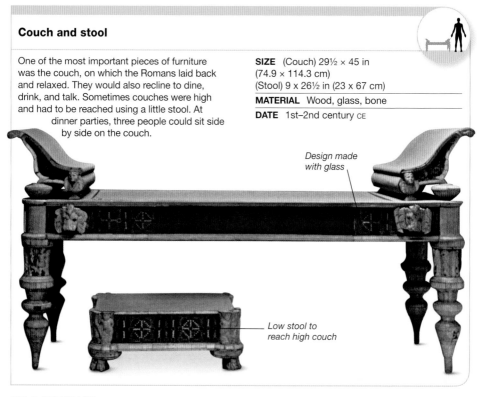

Design made with glass

Low stool to reach high couch

Bottles

The Romans used glass to make a variety of things. Neat glass bottles with handles held valuable liquids for trade, but when empty, they were used to store food in the kitchen, in the same way we reuse glass jars today. Jars of different sizes were also measuring devices.

Each bottle measures half the quantity of the larger one

SIZE Largest about 14 × 6½ in (36 × 17 cm)

MATERIAL Glass

DATE 1st century CE

Grinder

Stone grinders were used to crush foodgrains at home. The grain was ground between the lower fixed stone and the upper mobile stone, turned with the help of a handle.

SIZE About 14 in (35 cm)

MATERIAL Stone

DATE Reconstruction

Comb

The Romans used combs, like this one found from Ein Gedi, near the Dead Sea, to manage and style hair. The teeth of combs were cut with a very fine saw. This one has two rows of teeth—one fine and the other broader—to manage hair of different thicknesses.

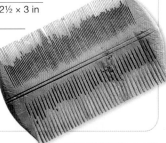

SIZE About 2½ × 3 in (6 × 8 cm)

MATERIAL Wood

DATE 2nd–3rd century CE

Lamp

Terra-cotta oil lamps were produced throughout the empire and were moulded into a variety of shapes. The circular area had a hole to pour in oil, usually olive oil. This lamp shows a gladiator in training.

Hole for wick _____

SIZE About 5½ × 3½ in (14 × 9 cm)

MATERIAL Terra-cotta

DATE 1st century CE

Ladle

A ladle, or *simpulum*, allowed the server to draw out wine or oil from a deep container. Priests also used it for religious ceremonies.

SIZE About 4 × 2½ in (10.5 × 6.5 cm)

MATERIAL Silver

DATE 1st century CE

Table

Roman tables were often decorated. This three-legged table, or *mensa*, was found in the House of the Faun in Pompeii. Its top has a star and vine-shoot motifs.

SIZE About 28 in (70 cm)

MATERIAL Bronze

DATE 1st century CE

Table legs often had clawed or hoofed ends

Hand mirror

Mirrored glass had not been invented in their times, so they used polished metal for the same purpose. They valued a well-groomed appearance and, hence, looking glass was important to them. Mirrors were hung in baths as well as other public places.

Wooden case for mirror

SIZE About 10 in (25 cm)
MATERIAL Canned copper, lead
DATE 2nd century CE

Saucepan

Bronze was widely used to make kitchen utensils because it cooked the food evenly. The copper content, however, could make some food unsafe to eat, even making them poisonous. To prevent that, the utensils were sometimes coated with less harmful metals such as silver and tin.

SIZE About 6 in (15 cm)
MATERIAL Bronze
DATE 1st century CE

Dressing up

Romans took care of their appearance. Men visited barbers and women had a morning beauty routine. Many accessories have survived. Fabrics decayed, but we know about them from paintings, statues, and carvings.

FOCUS ON...
MAKEUP
Roman women used many cosmetic products made from natural elements.

Toga

Free men wore a *toga*. It was a large piece of cloth, usually white, wrapped around the body and flung over the shoulder. Men of different ages and stations wore different types of *toga*.

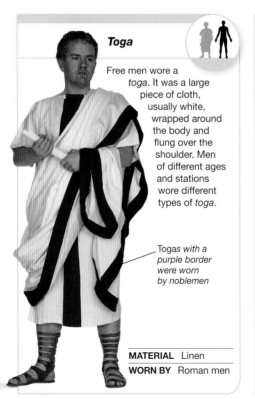

Togas *with a purple border were worn by noblemen*

MATERIAL   Linen
WORN BY   Roman men

Stola and *palla*

Women wore a *stola*, an ankle-length pleated dress, over the basic tunic. It was usually sleeveless and had two belts. Women might drape a shawl-like *palla* over the *stola*. Wealthy women would often have their clothes made from brightly patterned silks and cottons.

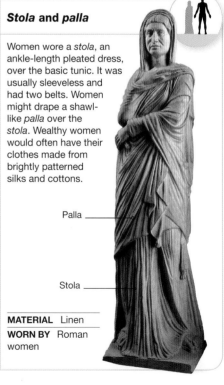

Palla

Stola

MATERIAL   Linen
WORN BY   Roman women

▲ Antimony was used to make *kohl*, which was applied to darken eyelashes and eyebrows.

▲ Ground red ocher pigment served as blush to redden cheeks and lips.

▲ Saffron was dusted over eyelids to be used as "eyeshadow."

Armlet

Romans were heavily inspired by the Greek style of goldwork. The snake was a popular motif in bracelets and armlets. This gold armlet, dating from 1st century CE, was found in Egypt.

MATERIAL	Gold
WORN BY	Men and women

Because the snake was the symbol of many deities, the snake armlet was believed to protect its wearer.

Snake head

Amulet

Young boys wore amulets, called *bullae*, around their neck. A *bulla*, such as the one below, was made with lead in gold foil. Some were, however, made with less precious materials.

MATERIAL Gold, lead

WORN BY Roman boys

Neck chain

Hairpins

Elaborate hairstyles for women came into fashion during the reign of Emperor Augustus. Hairpins were often needed to hold the hair in complex styles. Needles and pins were among the most common objects made from bone.

MATERIAL Copper, bone

WORN BY Roman women

Ring

Finger rings were worn as ornaments, but often served a practical purpose. For instance, some were seals and others were magic charms.

Cameo on gold ring

MATERIAL Gold, glass

WORN BY Men, women, children

Brooch

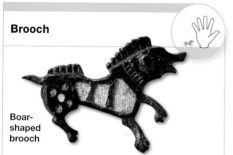

Boar-shaped brooch

The Romans used a *fibula*, or brooch, because their clothing was usually pinned at the shoulder rather than sewn. The *fibulae* were often elaborately decorated.

MATERIAL Bronze, enamel
WORN BY All Romans

Earrings

Many women had their ears pierced for earrings. Jewelry set with stones, rather than made of pure gold, was encouraged in the empire. Wealthy women would often also wear pearl earrings.

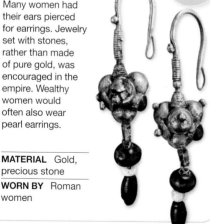

MATERIAL Gold, precious stone
WORN BY Roman women

Necklace

Emerald

Wealthy Romans wore jewelry made of precious metal and precious stones. As the empire flourished, Roman jewelry became more expensive and decorative. This 1st-century CE gold necklace was recovered from Pompeii.

MATERIAL Gold, emeralds, pearls
WORN BY Roman women

Medicine

HERBS
Romans knew many
medicinal plants and
used them in drugs
and ointments.

Romans learned a lot about medicines
from the ancient Greeks. Doctors
prepared ointments and could also
perform surgery. Opium was given
as a painkiller during the operations
and vinegar was used to clean wounds.

▲ Fenugreek seeds
were used to treat lung
diseases, particularly
pneumonia.

▲ Fennel was believed to
have calming properties.
It was given to people
with nervous disorders.

▲ Sage was sacred to the
Romans and was a cure
for many ailments, such
as indigestion.

Ointment jars

The person who made ointments was called
an *unguentarius* in ancient Rome. Ointments, for both
medical and cosmetic purposes, were commonly stored in
glass bottles known as *unguentaria*.

SIZE	Unavailable
MATERIAL	Glass
DATE	1st century CE

Medicine spoon

The Roman *cochleare* was a small spoon with a long handle and sharp end. A *cochleare* indicates a fixed measure of liquid. This measure was used to prescribe liquid medicines.

SIZE 6½ in (16.9 cm) long

MATERIAL Silver

DATE 1st century CE

Surgeon's knife

A surgeon's kit had various kinds of knife, and they all had a specific purpose. The knives usually had a bronze handle and a blade made of steel. They were cleaned in boiling water before use.

SIZE About 4 in (10 cm) long

MATERIAL Bronze, steel

DATE 1st century BCE–1st century CE

Extraction forceps

Roman doctors used forceps to extract splinters or bone fragments that were too small to be removed by hand. They also helped remove fractured skull pieces.

SIZE 8½ in (21 cm) long

MATERIAL Bronze

DATE 1st century CE

Squeezing handles closed these prongs

Fulcrum, or pivot

Elevator

The lever, or elevator, was used in Roman times to ease a bone back into its place when setting a fracture. It may have also been used to move teeth into their correct position.

SIZE About 4 in (10 cm) long

MATERIAL Bronze, silver

DATE 1st century CE

Ridged edge for better grip

Entertainment

Romans had many ways of filling their leisure hours. In addition to going to the baths or horse races, they might see mime performances at the theater, play dice games, or take part in one of the many of religious festivals.

Roman calendar showing dates of agricultural festivals

Street musician playing a double pipe

Festivals

There were many religious festivals in a year. Some were lively, such as Saturnalia in December, when there were parties and masters had to wait on their slaves.

Music and dance

Slaves or professional musicians, although generally not upper-class Romans, performed music and dance. They were part of religious festivals, the theater, and the arena. There were no concerts.

Theater

Although drama was less popular than the arena games, the largest theater in Rome could still hold 25,000 spectators. Mime, comedy, and dance were especially popular at the theater. Plays involving speech fell out of fashion.

Actors in masks

Tambourine was used mainly for religious purposes

Games

The Romans loved dice and board games. One very popular game was *duodecim scripta*, a version of modern backgammon. Most games involved some form of gambling.

Dice players

Toys and games

Ancient Romans of all ages enjoyed games and sports. Children's toys included dolls, model soldiers and animals, hoops and sticks, and marbles. Adults played games and gambled at bathhouses, taverns, and forums.

Ball game

This 1st-century CE fresco shows a group of young men playing with a ball. The ball was called a *pila*. Romans had many ball games, such as *harpastum* and *trigon*.

SIZE About 6 in (15 cm)

MATERIAL Leather

Pila

Dice

Cup to shake and roll dice

The Romans played dice by shaking them in a cup and then tossing them. Bets were placed on the outcome. Even legionaries played dice to entertain themselves.

SIZE One die about $1/3$ x $1/3$ x $1/3$ in (1 x 1 x 1 cm)

MATERIAL Bone, ivory

Board game

This game board from 1st–3rd century CE was meant for *ludus latrunculorum*, a strategy game like chess. Some historians believe that the game was based on army tactics.

SIZE $6\frac{1}{2}$ × $4\frac{3}{4}$ in (16 × 12 cm)

MATERIAL Concrete or stone

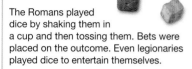

Counters

Puppet

Ancient Romans often placed dolls or puppets in the graves of children. This clay puppet of a soldier was found in a child's grave. The movement of the puppets was controlled by a rod that passed through a hole at the top of the head.

Some historians believe that the puppets were more than toys and were also used in theater.

SIZE Unavailable

MATERIAL Clay

The largest stadium for chariot racing in ancient Rome, the Circus Maximus, could seat

250,000 people

CHARIOT RACING

One of the most popular forms of entertainment in the Roman Empire, chariot racing was a dangerous sport. Racers could get badly hurt while trying to take turns at high speed. There were different kinds of chariot, depending on the number of horses drawing it—a *quadriga*, such as the one seen here, was pulled by four horses.

Music

Romans played music at the theater, at gladiatorial games, at dinner parties, in the streets, at religious ceremonies, and during funeral processions. The nobility took music and dance lessons, but they never performed professionally, because this was considered vulgar.

Water organ

This 3rd-century CE mosaic shows a *hydraulis*, or water organ. It was a popular instrument in Roman times. Water was used to compress air in a chamber. The player would press valves to release this air into pipes, producing musical notes.

MADE OF Wood, metal
SIZE 6½ × 3 ft (2 × 0.9 m)

Panpipes

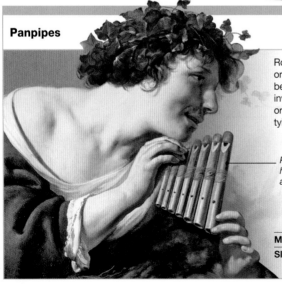

Romans adapted the panpipes, or pan flute, from the Greeks, who believed that the instrument was invented by the god Pan. *Fistula panis,* or the Roman panpipes, were made by tying together pipes of decreasing length.

Panpipes shown in the hands of the god Pan in a 17th-century painting

MADE OF Cane, wood, metal, stone
SIZE About 8 × 6 in (20 × 15 cm)

Double pipe

The two pipes, or tubes, of this wind instrument were blown into together to make music. The musicians who played this instrument were known as *tibicines*.

MADE OF Wood

SIZE About 1 ft (30 cm)

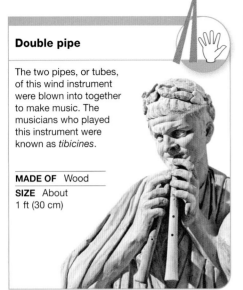

Cymbals

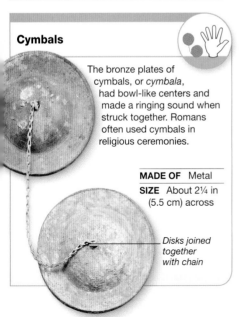

The bronze plates of cymbals, or *cymbala*, had bowl-like centers and made a ringing sound when struck together. Romans often used cymbals in religious ceremonies.

MADE OF Metal

SIZE About 2¼ in (5.5 cm) across

Disks joined together with chain

Lyre

This stringed instrument had the strings set in a curved, hollow body, similar to this reconstruction. The most popular form of lyre in ancient Rome was the professional instrument *kithara*.

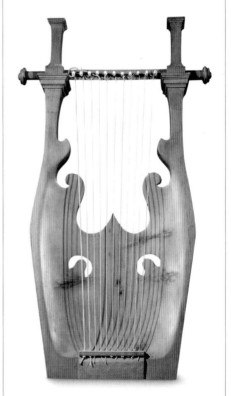

MADE OF Wood, metal

SIZE Unavailable

Arts and crafts

Works of art were valued greatly in Roman society. From public works, such as statues that glorified emperors, to wall paintings in the homes of the rich, arts and crafts played a prominent role.

Mosaic

Using small *tesserae* (cubes of colored marble or glass), skilled mosaic artists created images. Romans used mosaics mostly to decorate floors of palaces and villas. Mosaic artists offered "pattern books" from which people could select designs.

A Roman holding busts of ancestors

Sculpture

Roman sculpture was originally inspired by Greek models. Rich Romans paid sculptors to create statues of themselves or their family members. Friezes (horizontal sculpted bands) decorated buildings and monuments.

Glassware

Romans were masters at making glassware, particularly after the invention of glass blowing in about 50 BCE. Although colored glass was popular, the most expensive was clear glass used for tableware and luxury drinking vessels.

Glass vessel used at funerals

Decorative frame

Metalwork

Silver and gold-plated objects were luxury items. They were often engraved, sometimes with scenes from mythology and, in the later Roman Empire, with patterns of lines and shapes.

Silver mirror

Fresco

Almost all surviving Roman paintings are wall paintings made by applying colors (pigments) on carefully prepared plaster when its damp—a technique known as fresco. Many frescoes were preserved intact in the ruins of Pompeii.

Pink pigment made from madder plant

Red pigment

"Egyptian blue" pigment

Works of art

Art in the Roman Empire was influenced by artistic trends in other civilizations, such as those of the Greeks. From colorful mosaics to frescoes, stone carvings to cameos, art flourished in the Roman Empire.

FOCUS ON...
CRAFTSMEN AT WORK
Roman artisans were skilled in making a variety of artifacts.

Boar mosaic

The Romans decorated their walls and floors with mosaics created using tiny cubes of pottery, glass, or stone. As in this example, scenes from everyday life and common animals featured in mosaics.

DATE   Unknown

FROM   North Africa

▲ Smiths hammered different metals, such as copper, into shape at workshops similar to this one.

▲ Glass-makers made vessels by pressing hot glass into molds. Later, they learned to blow glass into shape.

▲ Stonemasons made carvings on stone that adorned many structures in Rome.

Silver goblet

Silver cups decorated with delicate designs were used by the rich for drinking wine. The design on this goblet shows skeletons of poets and philosophers, expressing the idea that even well-known people would eventually die and so life should be enjoyed to the full.

DATE 1st century CE

FROM Pompeii, Italy

Girl fresco

Frescoes are paintings made by applying paint to a layer of freshly laid lime plaster on a wall or ceiling. Since not many Roman women were educated, this fresco of a girl with a book is rare.

DATE c. 75 CE

FROM Pompeii, Italy

Cameo vase

Ancient Romans perfected the art of making elegant glassware using the cameo technique. This involved carving out designs through layers of multicolored glass. The Portland Vase shown here was used only by the royalty.

DATE 1st century CE
FROM Rome, Italy

Medusa mosaic

This detail of a floor mosaic features Medusa, a popular mythical figure who had snakes for hair. Ancient Romans believed that anyone who looked at her would turn into stone. Mythical subjects were commonly used by craftsmen to adorn the villas of the rich.

DATE
2nd–3rd century CE
FROM
Ephesus, Turkey

Glass *amphora*

Glass making reached its peak in the 2nd century CE. Adding metals gave the glass bright colors. Bands of the colored glass were used to make jars, such as this *amphora*. Romans used these vessels to store wine.

DATE 1st–2nd century CE
FROM Unavailable

Still-life fresco

Roman frescoes tell us a lot about the life and ways of the people living in those times. This fresco shows fruits in a glass bowl. Fruit was a common subject in Roman still life.

DATE 1st century CE

FROM Pompeii, Italy

Even a small mosaic is made up of thousands of tiny colored stones

LIFE IN MOSAIC
Roman mosaics often depicted different aspects of daily life. This mosaic from the 2nd century CE depicts theater masks—the female one represents tragedy and the male one, comedy. Theater actors wore masks to show the characters they were playing. Every mask bore a different expression.

At a glance

TECHNOLOGY

★ Central heating
Roman baths and villas were kept warm by an elaborate heating system known as a *hypocaust*. Wood was burned to create heat, which spread through inside the walls and under the floors of rooms.

★ Arches
The concrete arches that Romans built could bear twice the weight that a standard beam could carry.

★ Ropes
Romans would use hair from horses or even humans to make ropes that were both strong and stretchy—useful in catapults.

★ Metal glass
Romans knew the use of dichroic glass—glass with layers of different metals that can change color according to the angle of light. The 4th-century CE Lycurgus Cup, made with dichroic glass, turned from green to red.

★ Building crane
The drum crane was a machine that allowed just four workers to lift objects that weighed up to 4,000 lb (1,814 kg). This helped Romans build huge structures.

★ Glasswork
Craftsmen in ancient Rome used molds to shape molten glass quickly, a technique still used in today's glassblowing factories.

FESTIVALS

★ January 1
On this day, new consuls would officially join the Senate. Bulls were sacrificed to Jupiter to thank him for his protection during the past year.

★ February 13–21 (Parentalia)
During this festival, people honored their dead ancestors. Temples closed down, and weddings were forbidden.

★ August 13
A feast on this day was dedicated to goddess Diana. Slaves had the day off.

★ December 7–14 (Saturnalia)
Held in honor of the god Saturn, Saturnalia was the biggest festival of the year. Romans exchanged presents and at dinner parties the masters waited on the slaves.

DID YOU KNOW?

♦ When the Roman Empire reached its maximum size in 117 CE, it spanned about 2.5 million sq miles (6.5 million sq km).

♦ Spartacus, a slave who served as a gladiator, escaped and led a revolt against the Roman state. He built an army of 90,000 escaped slaves but was defeated and killed in 71 BCE.

♦ Romans troops had priority on the roads. Everyone else had to give way to them.

♦ People often secretly directed water pipes into their homes to avoid paying for water.

♦ Romans washed their dishes by rubbing them with sand, then rinsing them in clear water.

♦ Romans kept track of time with the help of a sundial or a water clock. In public places and private homes, officials known as *apparitores* announced the time.

♦ The city of Pompeii was completely buried under a thick layer of volcanic ash a volcanic eruption of Mt Vesuvius in 79 CE. When explorers discovered the site centuries later in 1748, , Pompeii lay almost intact.

♦ Romans sacrificed male animals to honor gods and female animals to honor goddesses.

♦ Male Roman actors wore brown or yellowish masks and female actors wore white masks.

♦ To guard its ranks from the enemy, each *centuria* had a password that was changed daily.

♦ Asparagus was considered a delicacy and kept frozen in the Alps to help preserve it for feasts and festivals.

♦ Roman soldiers would treat wounds using a mixture of honey, vinegar, and cobwebs. The spider silk made bandages strong and protective and also helped the healing process.

♦ Rich Romans had special slaves called *tabellarii* who delivered letters for them. They could cover distances of up to 25 miles (40 km) on foot or up to 50 miles (80 km) by cart in a day.

♦ Water shows were organized in arenas by flooding them. Romans acted out naval battles, often with real boats and even crocodiles.

The *trepan*, or drill, which Roman sculptors used to create their art was also used as a surgical instrument.

Numbers and letters

NUMERALS

Roman numerals were made of a combination of seven letters. The smaller number was added if it came after the bigger number and subtracted if it came before.

I	1	XXX	30
II	2	XL	40
III	3	**L**	50
IV	4	LX	60
V	5	LXX	70
VI	6	LXXX	80
VII	7	XC	90
VIII	8	**C**	100
IX	9	**D**	500
X	10	CM	900
XII	12	**M**	1,000
XX	20	MC	1,100

ALPHABET

The Roman alphabet is still used today for many languages, including English. It has come from the even earlier Phoenician alphabet. The letters changed over centuries and finally took their present shape with a few additions to the Roman letters.

Phoenician c. 900 BCE	Earliest Greek c. 750 BCE	Etruscan c. 650 BCE	Roman c. 500 BCE
	A		A
	B		B
			C
	Δ		D
	E		E
Y			F
I	Z		G
	H		H
⊕	Θ	⊗	I

Phoenician c. 900 BCE	Earliest Greek c. 750 BCE	Etruscan c. 650 BCE	Roman c. 500 BCE
⅄	Ж	Ж	K
ᒷ	Λ	↲	L
ᕼ	ᙏ	ᙏ	M
ㄚ	N	Ч	N
₮	Ξ	⊞	
O	O	O	O
⊃	Π	↿	P
ᙡ	M	M	

Phoenician c. 900 BCE	Earliest Greek c. 750 BCE	Etruscan c. 650 BCE	Roman c. 500 BCE
Φ	ϙ	ϙ	Q
ᐺ	P	ᐦ	R
W	Σ	ᔑ	S
✝	T	T	T
Y	Y	Y	V
Φ	Ϙ		
X	X	X	X
Ψ	Y		

ROMULUS CALENDAR

The Roman calendar changed several times. The first was the Romulus calendar (shown here), believed to have been developed by Rome's legendary founder. It had 304 days divided into 10 months. The later calendars had 12 months. The last one, the Julian Calendar, was introduced by Julius Caesar in 46 BCE. The best Roman philosophers, astronomers, and mathematicians of Caesar's time helped develop it.

Month	Days	Derived from
Martius	31	the god Mars
Aprilis	30	probably, Latin word meaning "to open"
Maius	31	the god Maia
Iunius	30	the god Juno
Quintilis	31	the Latin word meaning "five"
Sextilis	30	the Latin word meaning "six"
September	30	the Latin word meaning "seven"
October	31	the Latin word meaning "eight"
November	30	the Latin word meaning "nine"
December	30	the Latin word meaning "ten"

Glossary

Aerarium A Roman public treasury to store money safely. The term comes from the Latin sense of money.

Ambush A sudden surprise attack by people who are lying in wait secretly.

Amphitheater An oval arena, usually in the open air, where games and gladiator fights were staged.

Amphora A tall jar with a narrow neck and two handles, usually made of ceramic, clay, or glass and used to store liquids.

Antimony A shiny, silvery white metal-like substance that can easily break or shatter.

Aqueduct A channel (often either raised or buried) that carried water into Roman towns and cities.

Atrium The central hall or courtyard of a Roman *domus*. Most rooms opened to the *atrium*.

Aureus An ancient Roman gold coin equal to 25 Roman silver coins (*denarii*).

Auxiliary A soldier who served in the Roman army in a war but was not part of the regular army unit because he was not a Roman citizen.

Barracks A building or a group of buildings where soldiers are housed.

Basilica A large public building, usually located in a city's forum, used mainly as courthouse or for ceremonies.

Bireme An ancient galley (a warship powered by oars) that had two decks of oars, probably invented by the Phoenicians.

Bulla A good-luck charm worn by Roman boys.

Cameo A profile (side-view of the face) or a design carved or engraved in materials such as marble or stone, or more commonly on a piece of jewelry.

Cardo maximus The main north–south road that ran through Roman cities from which other roads branched out.

Celtic Related to the people and culture of places in Europe such as Scotland, Wales, Ireland, and Brittany.

Censor An official who kept a list of Roman citizens and also kept a watch on their behaviour.

Chi-rho A symbol of Christianity made of the first two letters of "Christ" in Greek—chi (X) and rho (P).

City-state A city that is independent and has its own government. It is not part of another country.

Consul A government official elected to keep a record of Roman citizens, issue contracts for roads and temples, and revise Senate membership.

Cult A popular religious group or belief that was different from the main religion. Cults were dedicated to the worship of a particular figure or god.

Denarius A silver coin used in ancient Roman currency.

Dictator A state official who was granted complete control by the Senate in times of crisis.

Diptych A pair of tablets that are hinged together so that the pair can be opened and closed like a book.

Domus A private family home in town, sometimes with shops, belonging to wealthy or upper-class Romans. It often had a garden in the back surrounded by columns.

Emperor The supreme ruler of all territories under the Roman Empire. "Emperor" was a higher rank than "king." The term was first used by Augustus Caesar.

Empire A large group of different regions that is ruled by an emperor or empress.

Equestrian A wealthy social class descended from the first cavalry officers of the Roman army. These Romans mostly owned their businesses and were not senators.

Etruscan People, language, or subject related to Etruria, an ancient region in western Italy between the Tiber and Arno rivers.

Forum The main market square in a Roman city, surrounded by public buildings. Public business and trade were conducted there.

Frontier The border, or boundary, of a country that separates it from other countries.

Garum A strong-tasting sauce made from fermented, salted fish.

Gaul An ancient region in Western Europe that included modern-day France, Belgium, southern Netherlands, southwestern Germany, and northern Italy.

Gladiator A trained fighter (usually a slave or a prisoner) who battled other gladiators—or wild animals—in contests until one of them died.

Hypocaust A central heating system developed in ancient Roman times in which hot air created by a fire flowed through cavities under floors and in walls.

Inscription Words or letters carved on a surface such as marble.

Insula A large apartment building of mainly rented accommodation.

Legion The main division of the Roman army. Each legion was made of 10 smaller units (cohorts).

Legionary A soldier in the Roman army from the plebeian class.

Milecastle A small rectangular fort built along a frontier, such as Hadrian's Wall, during the Roman Empire.

Mosaic A design or picture made with small pieces of stone, glass, or tile, usually cemented in a wall or floor.

Oculus A round window or opening, usually in a dome.

Papyrus An Egyptian water reed that was pressed into sheets that were used to write on. Later, Romans also used them for writing.

Patrician A person belonging to a noble family or class who was an ancient Roman citizen.

Pediment A triangular feature on the front of a building, usually built above a portico of columns or a door, window, or other opening.

Peristyle A garden surrounded by columns and often found behind a grand Roman house.

Persecute To oppress or mistreat people.

Pigment A natural coloring material obtained from rocks, animals, or plants.

Plebeian A Roman citizen who was a member of the ordinary working class.

Praetor A high-ranking, elected judge in the Roman state.

Province Roman territory that was outside Italy. The people who lived there were called "provincials."

Quadriga A Roman chariot that was drawn by four horses.

Quaestor An elected government official who had to take care of the state's finances.

Relief A carved or molded picture that stands out from its background.

Republic A type of government in ancient Rome designed to stop any one individual from becoming too powerful. Under the Republic, Rome was governed by two elected leaders who ruled for just a year.

Samnite People from the region called Samnium in south-central Italy. Samnium was much bigger in Roman times than it is today.

Shrine A holy place for worship, associated with a sacred figure or relic.

Slave A man, woman, or child who is owned by another person as property, usually to do some kind of work.

Standard A flag or small statue that is the emblem of an organization, often an army or military unit.

Testudo Meaning "tortoise," a protective formation of Roman troops. Soldiers held shields above their heads in a way that the shields overlapped.

Tetrarchy A form of government led by four rulers.

Thermopolium A food and wine stall in Roman times similar to a tavern. It served wine and ready-made hot food to customers.

Triumvir A Roman official of the triumvirate—a political unit with three officials in charge of it.

Tympanum A triangular space set into a wall, often with a carved stone panel.

Urban An area such as a city or town where lots of people live together in close-set buildings.

Vexillum A flag bearing the standard of a Roman legion.

Villa A wealthy family's luxurious country house, often on a farming estate.

Index

AB

aerarium 15
agriculture 115, 117
 festivals 130
Agrippina 20
Alaric 65
Alcántara Bridge (Spain) 108
Alesia, Battle of 59, 63
alphabet 118, 148–9
Amphitheater of El Jem 103
amphitheaters 39, 102–7
amphorae 11, 143
amulets 126
Ancient Romans 14–39
antimony 125
Antoninus Pius 7, 22
Antony, Mark 19, 63
Apollo 72
Aqueduct of the Miracles
 (Mérida) 111
Aqueduct of Segovia 108
aqueducts 81, 108–11
arches 81, 87, 146
architecture 81, 86–7
Arena of Nîmes 105
arenas 102–7, 147
Arminius 64
armlets 125
armor 48–51
army 28–9, 41, 42–3, 147
arts and crafts 138–45
asparagus 147
Augustus 6, 7, 15, 19, 94
aureus 11
auxiliaries 16
Bacchus 74, 90
backpacks 51
bakers 116

ball games 132
ballista 47
baths 100–1, 130
Baths of Trajan (Rome) 101
battles 56–9
belts 49
bireme 53
board games 131, 133
bottles 121
Boudica 64–5
bows and arrows 44
bricks 91
bridges 81, 108–11
Britain 26–7, 64–5
bronze tablets 119
brooches 127
Brutus, Lucius Junius 30
Brutus, Marcus Junius 33
building materials 91
building tools 87, 146
buildings and monuments
 80–111

C

Caesar, Julius 6, 18, 32, 33, 63
calendars 130, 149
Caligula 20
cameos 140, 142
Camillus, Marcus Furius 30
caravans 84
Carthaginians 5, 55, 58, 62
Cato the Elder 32
Cato the Younger 32–3
cavalry 42, 43, 48
central heating 146
centuria 43
Ceres 75
chariot racing 134–5

Charon 67
children 16, 114–5
 as slaves 36
Christianity 8, 69
Cicero 34
Circus Maximus (Rome)
 103, 134
circuses 102
cities 82–3
citizens 15, 16, 42
civil wars 6, 55
class structure 17
Claudius 7, 20
Cleopatra VII 19, 63
clothing 124
cohorts 43
coinage 11
Colosseum (Rome) 102–3,
 106–7
combs 121
comedy 131
concrete 91
conquests 5, 7, 41
Constantine I 8, 24–5, 69
consuls 146
contubernium 43
coolus 49
corona triumphalis 18
couches 120
craftsmen 141
cranes 11, 146
Crassus, Marcus
 Licinius 32–3
cults 69, 79
cymbals 137

DE

Dacian Wars 60–1
Dacians 40, 41, 54
daily life 114–5
dance 130, 131

denarius 11
Diana 66, 67, 72, 146
dice 130, 131, 133
Diocletian 8, 24
Diocletian's Palace (Split) 99
dishwashing 147
doctors 116
domes 86–7, 96–7
domus 89
double pipes 137
drama 131
earrings 127
Edessa, Battle of 59
elevators 129
emperors 7, 8, 15, 17, 18–25
enemies 62–5
engineering
    architectural 86
    military 43
entertainment 130–1
equestrians 17
Etruscans 5, 54, 56
extraction forceps 129

F

Fabricius's Bridge (Rome) 108
face masks 48, 131, 144–5, 147
families 16
fennel 128
fenugreek seeds 128
festivals 130, 146
flamines 68
Flora 76
food 41, 115, 147
forts 43
Fortuna 147
Forum Baths (Pompeii) 101
fountains 81

Franks 9
freedmen 17, 37
frescoes 120, 139, 141, 143
friezes 138
furniture 120–3

GHI

Gallic Wars 59
games 131, 132–3
    gladiatorial 38–9, 106–7
Garni Temple (Kotayk) 93
garum 115
generals 28–9
Germanic Wars 58–9
gladiators 38–9
gladius 45
glassware 139, 141, 142, 146
gods 67, 70–7
Goths 9, 65
Great Bath (Bath) 100
Greek influence 86, 138, 140
grid patterns 82
grinders 121
Hadrian 22
Hadrian's Villa (Tivoli) 98
Hadrian's Wall 26–7
hairpins 126
Hamilcar Barca 62
hand mirrors 123, 139
Hannibal 28, 58, 62
harvesting 117
hasta 45
helmets 49, 50–1
Heraclea, Battle of 57
herbs 115, 128
Herculaneum 89
homes 88–9

houses
    architecture 88–9
    furniture and artifacts 120–3
    gods 68
hygiene 100
Imperial Baths (Trier) 101
industry 11
inkwells 118
insignia 48
instruments
    musical 136–7
    surgical 129, 147
insulae 88, 89
invasions 9
Isis 69, 75

JKL

Jerusalem 55
jewelry 125–7
Juno 68, 70
Jupiter 68, 70, 90, 93, 146
Justinian 9
kings of Rome 4
kitchen equipment 120–3
ladles 122
lamps 122
language 113
Lares 68
Latin 6, 113
Latins 5, 54
leg guards 48
legions 42, 43, 48
Leptis Magna 87
Leptis Magna Theater 104–5
Les Ferreres Aqueduct (Tarragona) 110
letters 147
leveling staffs 87

Livia 19, 94
lyres 137

MNO

Maison Carrée (Nîmes) 92
makeup 125
manacles 37
marble 91
Marcellus, Marcus Claudius 31
Marcus Aurelius 23
Marius, Gaius 29
Mars 71
masks
    auxiliary cavalry 48
    theatrical 131, 144–5,
    147
Maxentius 55
medicine 128–9, 147
Mercury 77
metal glass 146
metal jackets 49
metalwork 139, 141
military 40–65
Milvian Bridge, Battle of 55
mime 131
Minerva 68, 71
Mithras 69, 76, 76–7, 93
Mithridates VI 63
months 149
monuments see buildings
    and monuments
mosaics 52–3, 98, 99, 120,
    138, 140, 142, 144–5
music 130, 136–7

NO

navy 53
necklaces 127
neighbors 5
Neptune 71

Nero 21
Nîmes 92, 105, 109
nobles 30–3
numerals 148
Octavian see Augustus
oculus 96
ointment jars 128
olive oil 100
opium 128
orators 17, 34
Ostia 83, 89
Ovid 34

P

palaces 81, 98–9
palla 124
Palmyra 84–5, 92–3
panpipes 136
Pantheon (Rome) 86–7, 91,
    96–7
papyrus 118
Parentalia 146
Park of Aqueducts (Rome) 109
Penates 69
pens 119
Persians 54, 59
philosophers 17, 34–5
pilum 46
pirates 53
plebeians 16, 17
plumbata 45
Plutarch 17
poets 17, 34–5
Pompeii 81, 89, 90, 98,
    101, 139
    Amphitheater 104
Pompey 29
Pont du Gard (Nîmes) 109
Pont Julien (France) 108
provincial cities 83, 84–5
Ptolemy 35

pugio 46
Pula Arena 104
Punic Wars 28, 53,
    55, 58, 62
puppets 133
purple dye 18
Pyrrhic War 57

R

rations, army 41
red ocher 125
reed pens 119
religion 66–79
    festivals 130, 146
rings 126
roads 10, 12–13
Roman Empire 6–9
    division of 9
    expansion of 7, 54, 55
    territorial extent 147
Roman life 112–45
Roman Republic 4–5, 6, 16
Roman–Etruscan Wars 56
Roman–Persian Wars 59
Rome, city of 82–3
Romulus and Remus 4
ropes 146
royal symbols 18

S

Sack of Rome 65
sacrifices 68–9, 146, 147
saffron 125
sage 128
Samnite Wars 57
Samnites 5, 39, 54
sandals 50–1
Saturn 76, 146
Saturnalia 146
saucepans 123

Scipio Africanus 28
sculpture 138
Senate 5, 18
senators 4–5, 17
Seneca 17, 21, 35
Septimius Severus 23
sesterius 11
shields 50
ships 10–11, 52–3
shopkeepers 117
silver goblets 141
slaves 17, 36–7, 147
society 15, 16–17
soldiers 42–3
Spartacus 147
spatha 46
spoons, medicine 129
Stilicho 9
stola 124
stonemasons 141
stools 120
strigils 100
stylus 119
Sulla 29
surgeon's knives 129

T

tabellarii 147
tables 122
tactics, military 42
Tarquinius Superbus 4
technology 146
Temple of Augustus and
   Livia (Vienne) 94
Temple of Bacchus
   (Baalbek) 90
Temple of Bel (Palmyra) 92–3
Temple of Jupiter (Pompeii) 90
Temple of Jupiter (Sbeitla) 93
Temple of Venus Genetrix
   (Rome) 95

Temple of Venus and Roma
   (Rome) 94–5
Temple of Zeus (Aizanoi) 95
temples 81, 86–7, 90–7
tesserae 37
testudo formation 42–3
tetrarchy 8
Teutoburg Forest, Battle
   of the 64
Theater of Aphrodisias
   (Karacasu) 102
theaters 103, 131
Theodosius I 25
thinkers 17, 34–5
Thracians 39
Tiber River 83
timekeeping 147
togas 124
town plans 82
toys 132–3
trade 10–11, 84
Trajan 7, 22, 60–1
Trajan's Column 60–1
transportation 10–11
treasury 15
triangles 87

UVWZ

uniform, military 48–51
units, army 43
Uthina Amphitheater 105
Valens Aqueduct
   (Istanbul) 110
Valentinian I 25
Valerian 59
Vandals 9
vases 142
Venus 72, 73, 94, 95
Vercingetorix 59, 63
Vespasian 21

vexillum 48
Villa of the Mysteries
   (Pompeii) 98
Villa Romana del Casale
   (Sicily) 99
villas 88, 89, 98–9
vinegar 128
Virgil 17, 34–5
Volscians 54
Volubilis 83
Vulcan 73
wars 41, 54–61
water organs 136
water shows 147
water supplies 108–11,
   120, 147
weapons 44–5
women 16, 114
work 116–17
writing 118–19
Zenobia 65

Acknowledgments

Dorling Kindersley would like to thank: Lorrie Mack for proofreading; Helen Peters for indexing; and Dhirendra Singh for design assistance.

The publishers would also like to thank the following for their kind permission to reproduce their photographs:

(Key: a-above; b-below/bottom; c-center; f-far; l-left; r-right; t-top)

1 **Dreamstime.com:** Ron Chapple (c). **2-3 Dreamstime.com:** Goran Bogicevic (c). **4 The Bridgeman Art Library:** The Stapleton Collection (bl). **4-5 Getty Images:** De Agostini (c). **5 Alamy Images:** The Art Archive (tr). **Dreamstime.com:** Perseomedusa (c). **6 Getty Images:** De Agostini. **7 Alamy Images:** Prisma Archivo (br). **Corbis:** Araldo de Luca (tl). **8 Dreamstime.com:** Kuvona (cl). **Getty Images:** De Agostini (bc). **9 Getty Images:** De Agostini (b); UIG (tl). **10 The Bridgeman Art Library:** Roman (cl). **Dorling Kindersley:** Courtesy of the National Maritime Museum, London (b). **11 Dreamstime.com:** Gavran333 (tr); Chris Hill (cr). **Getty Images:** De Agostini (br). **12-13 Corbis:** Lindsay Hebberd. **14 Getty Images:** De Agostini. **15 Getty Images:** De Agostini. **16 Alamy Images:** Interfoto (cl). **16-17 Alamy Images:** The Art Archive (b). **17 Alamy Images:** Interfoto (cl). **18 Fotolia:** picsfive (bl). **Getty Images:** DEA/C. Bevilacqua (bc). **19 Alamy Images:** The Art Archive (bc). **Corbis:** Bettmann (cla). **Getty Images:** DEA/S. Vannini (cra). **20 Alamy Images:** Prisma Archivo (tr). The Art Archive/Alfredo Dagli Orti (tl). **Getty Images:** The Bridgeman Art Library (bl). **21 Alamy Images:** The Art Archive (bl). **Corbis:** Bettmann (tl). **22 Dreamstime.com:** Alessandro0770 (bc). **Getty Images:** B&Y Photography Inc. (br); The Bridgeman Art Library/Roman (cr). **24 Getty Images:** Etc Ltd (bl). **24-25 Photoshot:** (c). **25 Alamy Images:** Jerónimo Alba (br). **Corbis:** Michael Nicholson (tc). **26-27 Alamy Images:** Izel Photography. **28 Getty Images:** DEA/G. Nimatallah. **29 Alamy Images:** The Art Gallery Collection. **Getty Images:** Saverio Altamura (tr); (br). **30 Corbis:** Araldo de Luca (bl). **Photo SCALA, Florence:** courtesy of Musei Civici Fiorentini (br). **31 The Bridgeman Art Library:** Alinari. **32 Alamy Images:** The Art Gallery Collection (tl). **The Bridgeman Art Library:** Alinari (cl). **33 Corbis:** Alinari Archives (tr). **Getty Images:** De Agostini (b). **34 Alamy Images:** Interfoto (tr). **Getty Images:** Roman (bl). **35 Alamy Images:** The Art Archive (c). **Corbis:** Roger Wood (bl). **Getty Images:** (br). **36 Getty Images:** DEA/A. Dagli Orti (c). **36-37 Alamy Images:** Ancient Art & Architecture Collection Ltd (c). **37 Alamy Images:** The Art Archive (cr). **Dorling Kindersley:** John Chase/Courtesy of the Museum of London (tc). **Photo SCALA, Florence:** courtesy of the Ministero Beni e Att. Culturali (tr). **38 Corbis:** Alinari Archives. **39 Dorling Kindersley:** Christi Graham and Nick Nicholls/The Trustees of the British Museum (bc). **40 Getty Images:** DEA/A. Dagli Orti. **42 akg-images:** Interfoto (cl). **42-43 Dreamstime.com:** Regien Paassen (b). **43 Dreamstime.com:** Andreas Weber (t). **44 Alamy Images:** stephen Mulcahey (bl). **45 Dorling Kindersley:** Ermine Street Guard (cl, tr). **Andreas Pangerl, www.romancoins.info:** (bl). **46 Alamy Images:** Interfoto (tr). **Dorling Kindersley:** Ermine Street Guard (l, br). **47 Alamy Images:** Jack Sullivan. **48 Dorling Kindersley:** University Museum of Newcastle (br). **Getty Images:** DEA/A. Dagli Orti

(cl); Universal Images Group (cla). **49 Dorling Kindersley:** Ermine Street Guard (cla, tr); University Museum of Newcastle (bc). **50 Alamy Images:** Travel Pictures (br). **Dorling Kindersley:** Ermine Street Guard (bl). **51 Dorling Kindersley:** Ermine Street Guard (tl, br). **52-53 Alamy Images:** The Art Archive. **54 Getty Images:** De Agostini (tl); DEA/A. Dagli Orti (bl). **55 Alamy Images:** Prisma Archivo (b). **Getty Images:** UIG (tr). **56 Alamy Images:** The Art Gallery Collection. **57 akg-images:** Erich Lessing (bl). **Alamy Images:** The Art Archive (tr). **58 Alamy Images:** The Art Archive (t). **58-59 Alamy Images:** The Art Archive (b). **59 The Bridgeman Art Library:** Giraudon (t). Corbis: (br). **60-61 Getty Images:** UIG. **62 Alamy Images:** Peter Horree (br); The Art Gallery Collection (cl). **63 Alamy Images:** Peter Horree (cla). **Dorling Kindersley:** Rough Guides/Angus Osborn (br). **64 Getty Images:** AFP (bl). **64-65 Dreamstime.com:** Vladimir Korostyshevskiy (c). **65 Alamy Images:** Mary Evans Picture Library (br); Peter Horree (tr). **66 Alamy Images:** The Art Archive. **67 Getty Images:** DEA/A. De Gregorio (bc). **68 Getty Images:** De Agostini (b). **68-69 Getty Images:** De Agostini (b). **69 Getty Images:** De Agostini (br); Mondadori Portfolio (tr). **70 Alamy Images:** Steve Vidler (bl); The Art Archive (cra). **71 Alamy Images:** The Print Collector (ca). **72 Getty Images:** (bl, br). **72 Alamy Images:** Sites & Photos (tl). **Dreamstime.com:** Vladimir Korostyshevskiy (tc). **Getty Images:** The Bridgeman Art Library/Roman (br). **73 Corbis:** Arte & Immagini srl (br). **74 Alamy Images:** Sonia Halliday Photographs. **75 Corbis:** Araldo de Luca (b). **Getty Images:** DEA/G. Dagli Orti (tr). **76 Alamy Images:** The Art Archive (b). **Corbis:** The Art Archive/Alfredo Dagli Orti (br). **Dorling Kindersley:** Rough Guides/Michelle Grant (cra). **77 Getty Images:** DEA/G. Nimatallah. **78-79 Getty Images:** UIG. **80 Corbis:** Eurasia Press/Steven Vidler. **81 Getty Images:** Roy Rainford (bc). **82 Corbis:** Araldo de Luca. **83 Corbis:** Ttatty (tl); Typhoonski (b). **84-85 Alamy Images:** Dario Bajurin. **87 Dreamstime.com:** Pascalou95 (tr). **88 Getty Images:** De Agostini (cr, br). **88-89 Getty Images:** SuperStock (b). **89 Alamy Images:** Bildagentur-online/Sunny Celeste (tr). **Corbis:** Araldo de Luca (tc). **Getty Images:** UIG (tl). **90 Alamy Images:** The Art Archive (bl). **Dreamstime.com:** Dinosmichail (cr). **91 Alamy Images:** VPC Travel Photo (tc). **Dreamstime.com:** Andre Nantel (t). **Fotolia:** fabiomax (b). **92-93 Dreamstime.com:** Witr (c). **93 Corbis:** Bob Krist (br). **Dreamstime.com:** Marcin Ciesielski/Sylwia Cisek (cra). **94 Corbis:** Atlantide Phototravel (tr). **94-95 Dreamstime.com:** Ekaterinabelova (b). **95 Corbis:** Arthur ThÉvenart (tl). **Dreamstime.com:** Evgeniy_p (br). **96-97 Alamy Images:** Sites & Photos. **98 Dorling Kindersley:** Rough Guides/Karen Trist (br). **99 Alamy Images:** Bosiljka Zutich (br). **Getty Images:** DEA Picture Library (bl). **100 Dreamstime.com:** Justin Black (br). **Getty Images:** De Agostini (bl). **101 Corbis:** Vanni Archive (b). **Dreamstime.com:** Travelpeter (cr). **Getty Images:** DEA/G. Dagli Orti (tl). **102 Dreamstime.com:** Valery Shanin (bl). **102-103 Dreamstime.com:** Wouter Tolenaars. **103 Getty Images:** Gelia (br). **104 Getty Images:** Ian Gethings (cl). **104-105 Getty Images:** Nico Tondini (t). **105 Corbis:** Keren Su (cr). **106-107 Dreamstime.com:** Ralf Siemieniec. **108 Alamy Images:** Robert Harding Picture Library Ltd (cla). **Dreamstime.com:** Lianem (cl); Richard Semik (bl); Typhoonski (br). **109 Alamy Images:** Vito Arcomano (t). **110 Dreamstime.com:** Mikhail Markovskiy (b);

Natursports (t). **111 Dreamstime.com:** Erlire. **112 Alamy Images:** The Art Archive. **113 Alamy Images:** Ashley Cooper (bc). **114 Getty Images:** De Agostini (cl). **114-115 Getty Images:** De Agostini (b). **115 Corbis:** Roger Wood (cr). **Dreamstime.com:** Witold Krasowski (tl). **116 Getty Images:** De Agostini (cl, br). **117 Getty Images:** De Agostini (tl, b). **118 Alamy Images:** The Art Archive (bl). **119 Getty Images:** DEA/A. Dagli Orti (t); (bl, br). **120 Corbis:** Francis G. Mayer (cl). **121 Alamy Images:** www.BibleLandPictures.com (br). **Getty Images:** De Agostini (tr). **122 Alamy Images:** The Art Archive (cl). **Getty Images:** De Agostini (cra); DEA/L. Pedicini (bc). **123 Alamy Images:** The Art Archive (b). **The Bridgeman Art Library:** Israel Antiquities Authority (tl). **124 akg-images:** Gilles Mermet (br). **125 Corbis:** Araldo de Luca (c). **Dreamstime.com:** Erickn (tc). **126 Alamy Images:** Interfoto (br); The Art Archive (tr). **127 Alamy Images:** Interfoto (bl); The Art Archive (tr). **Getty Images:** Gallo-Roman (c). **128 Dreamstime.com:** Trgowanlock (cl). **Getty Images:** De Agostini (b). **129 akg-images:** Museum Kalkriese (tr). **The Bridgeman Art Library:** Photo © Heini Schneebeli (tl); De Agostini (bl); Danita Delimont (tr). **130 Getty Images:** De Agostini (tl). **130-131 Getty Images:** De Agostini (t). **131 Getty Images:** De Agostini (tr); (br). **132 Alamy Images:** The Art Archive. **133 Alamy Images:** Prisma Archivo (tl). **Dreamstime.com:** Carlos Mora (bl). **Getty Images:** UIG (cr). **134-135 Getty Images:** DEA/G. Dagli Orti. **136 Getty Images:** Paulus Moreelse (bl); Roman (tc). **137 Alamy Images:** The Art Archive (t). **Getty Images:** DEA/A. De Gregorio (bl). **138 Alamy Images:** The Art Archive (tl). **138-139 Alamy Images:** CuboImages srl (b). **139 Alamy Images:** The Art Archive (br). **Getty Images:** DEA/L. Pedicini (c). **140 Alamy Images:** Ancient Art & Architecture Collection Ltd. **141 Alamy Images:** The Art Gallery Collection (bl). **Getty Images:** De Agostini (tl, tr); Roger Viollet (tc); UIG (cr). **142 Alamy Images:** Sonia Halliday Photographs (bl). **Corbis:** (tr). **Getty Images:** De Agostini (tl). **143 Alamy Images:** Sites & Photos. **144-145 Getty Images:** De Agostini

Jacket images: *Front:* **Dorling Kindersley:** Ermine Street Guard fcl/ (Helmet), cl/ (Dagger), crb/ (Military Sandals), crb/ (Knife), fclb/ (Knife), crb/ (Shield), crb/ (Helmet), bl/ (Dagger), br/ (Belt), Museo Archeologico Nazionale di Napoli bl/ (Sculpture), Rough Guides / Michelle Grant bl/ (Statue), The Natural History Museum, London crb/ (Brooch), University Museum of Newcastle fcr/ (Metal Chest), clb/ (Knee Guards), Ure Museum of Greek Archaeology, University of Reading fclb/ (Sandals); **Dreamstime.com:** Gavran333 crb/ (Leather pouch); *Back:* **Dorling Kindersley:** Ermine Street Guard clb/ (Shield), cl/ (Helmet), University Museum of Newcastle clb/ (Metal Chest)

All other images © Dorling Kindersley

For further information see:
www.dkimages.com